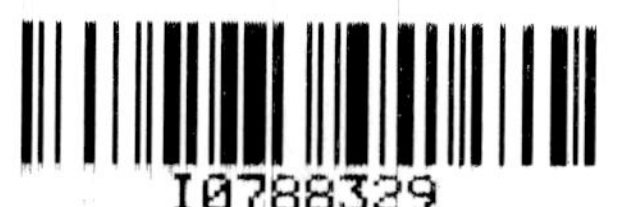


# Coloring book for adults and kids amazing donkey image for design

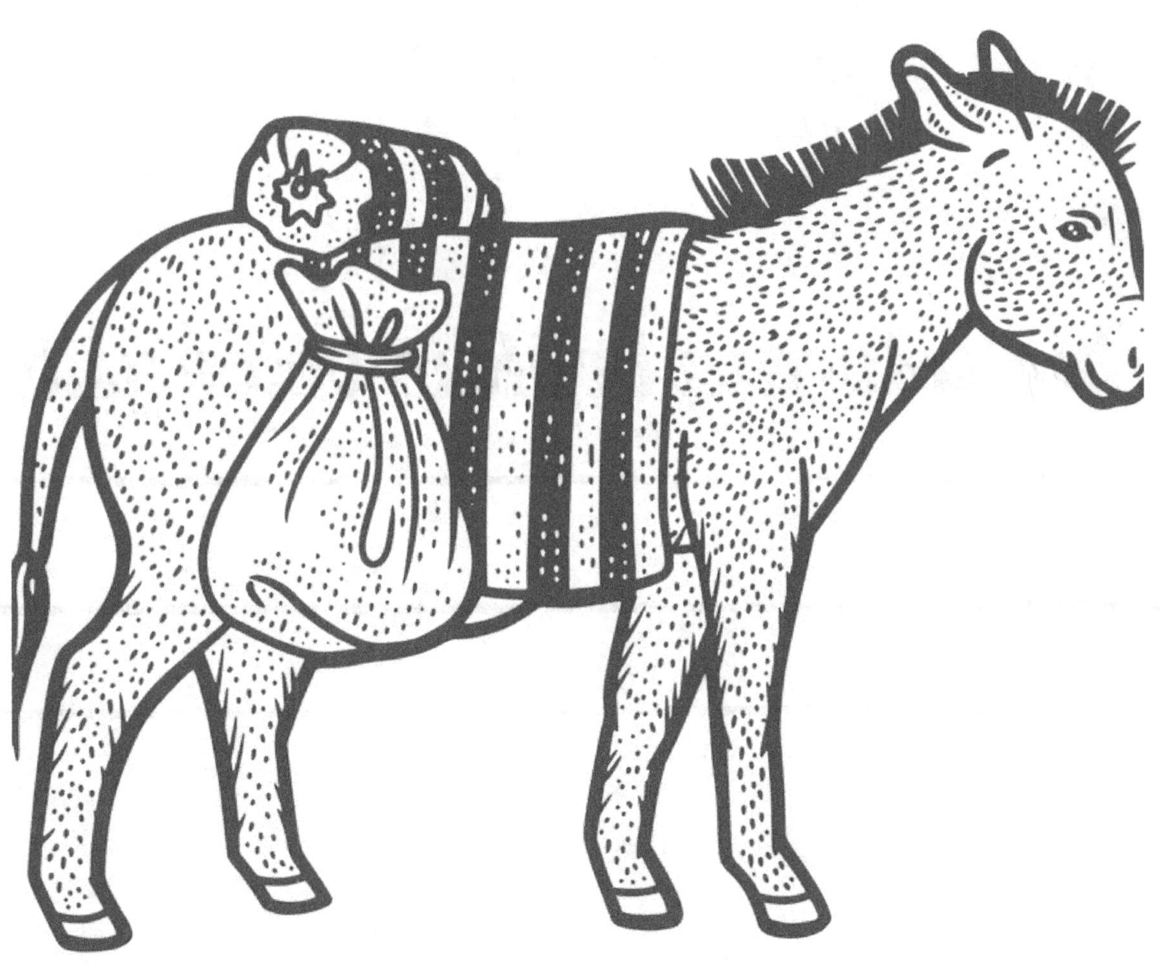

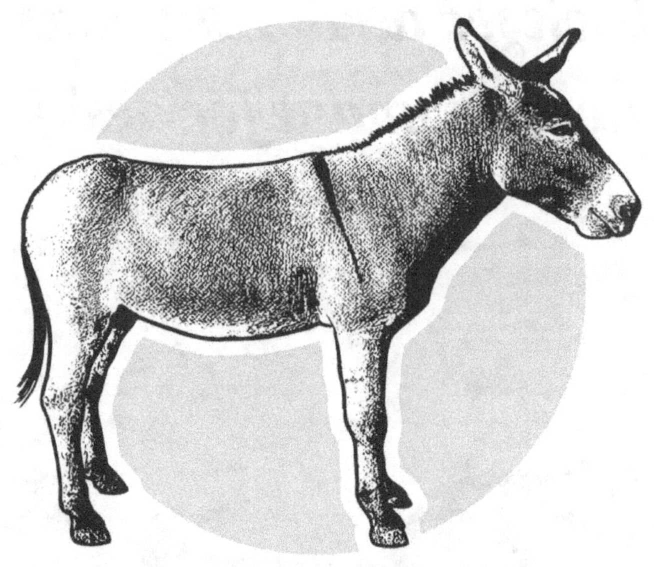

# This coloring book is belongs to

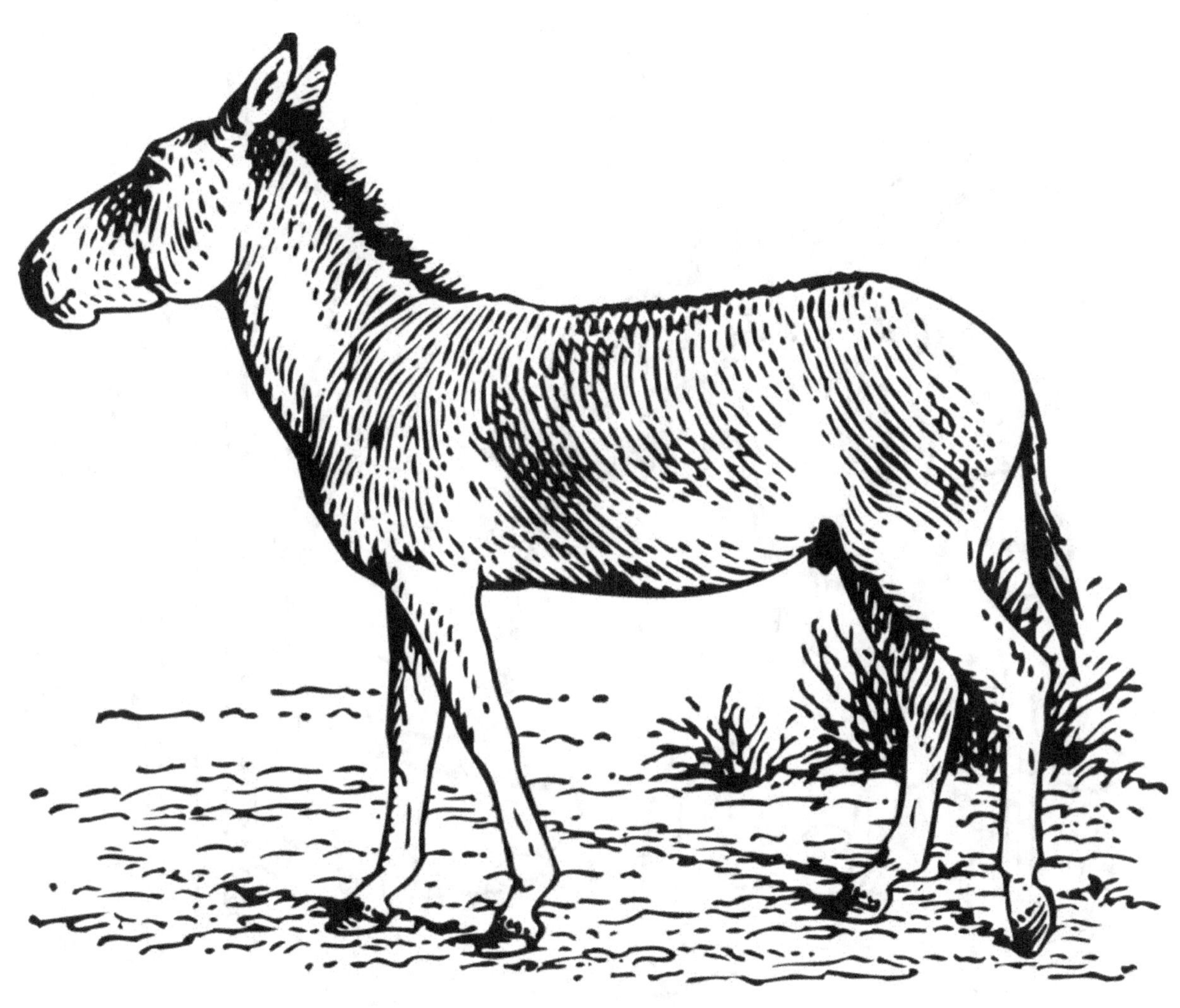

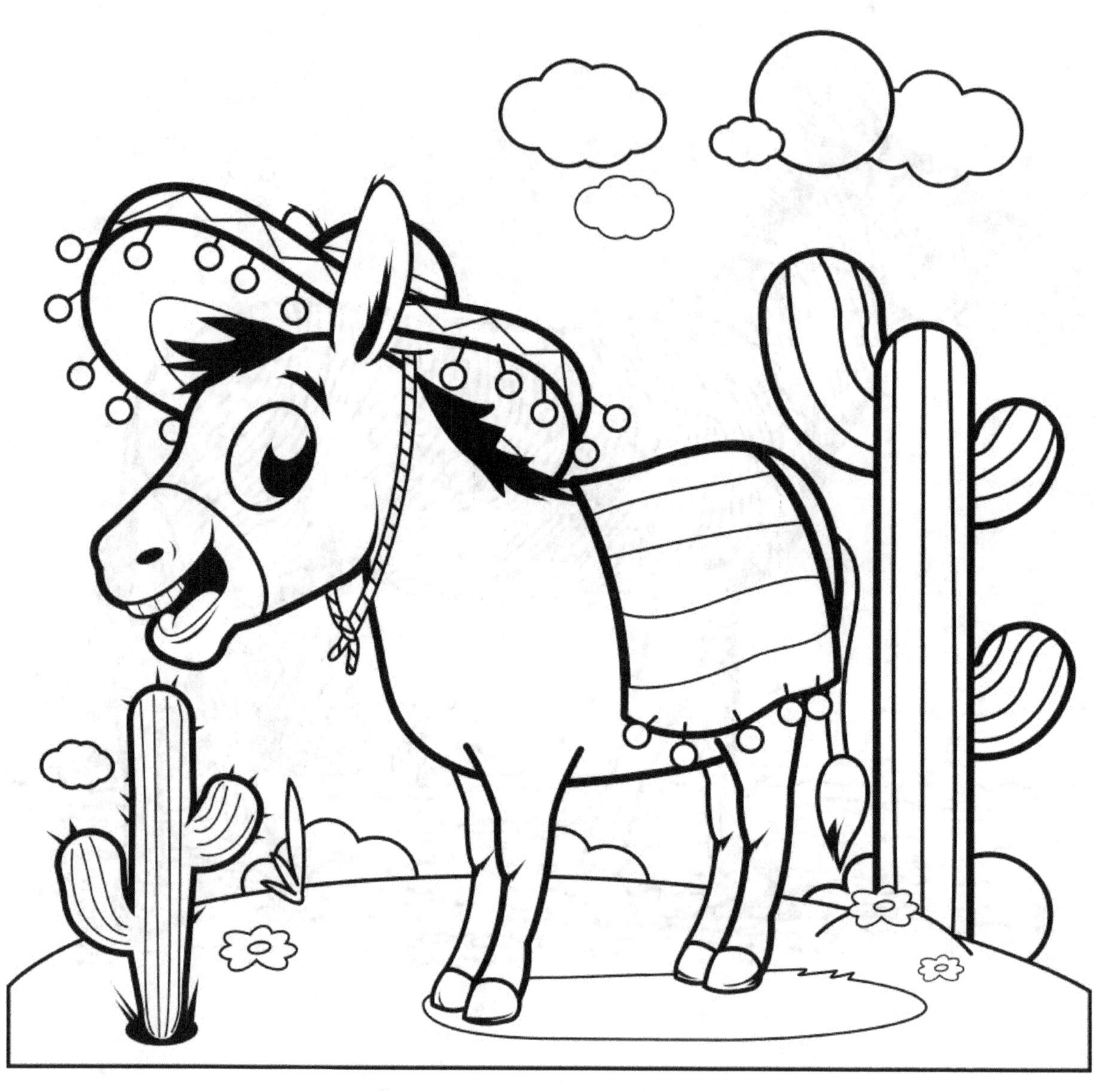

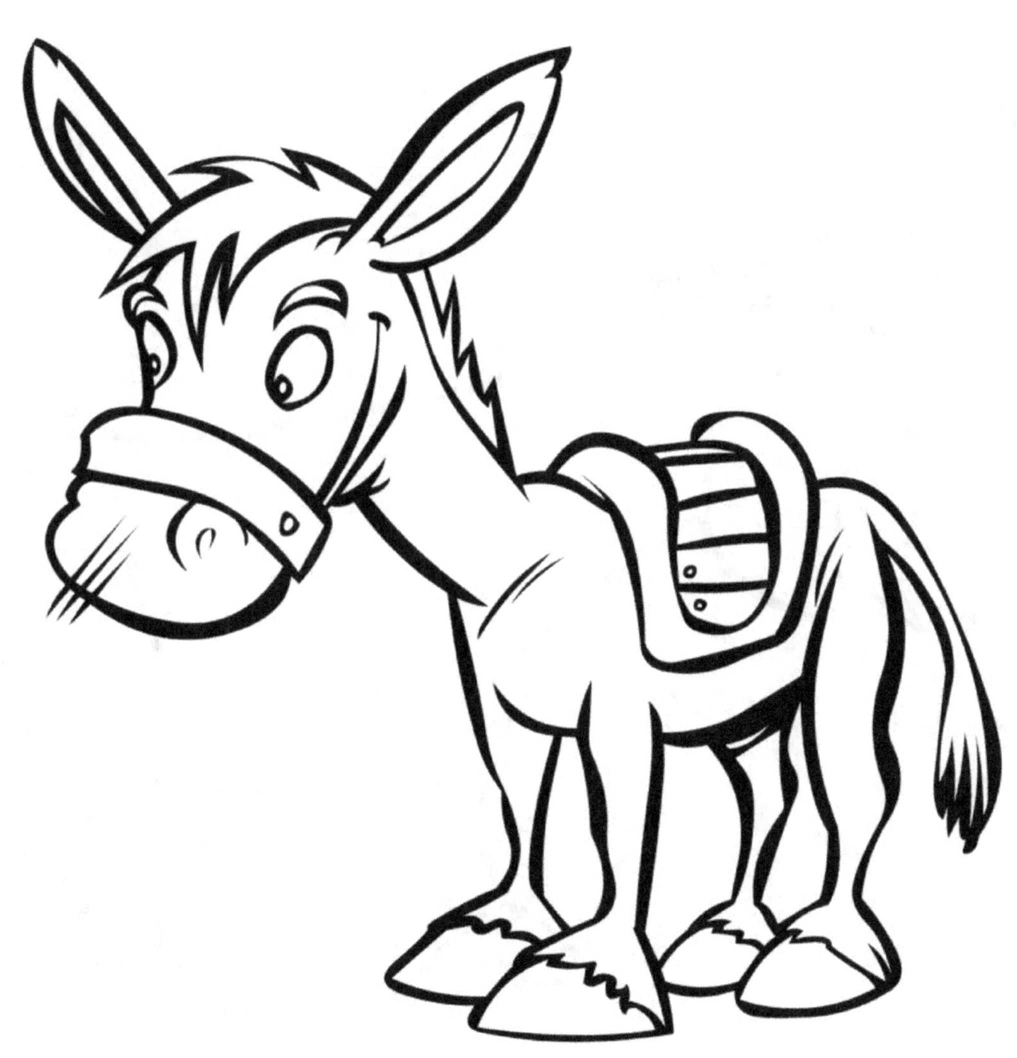

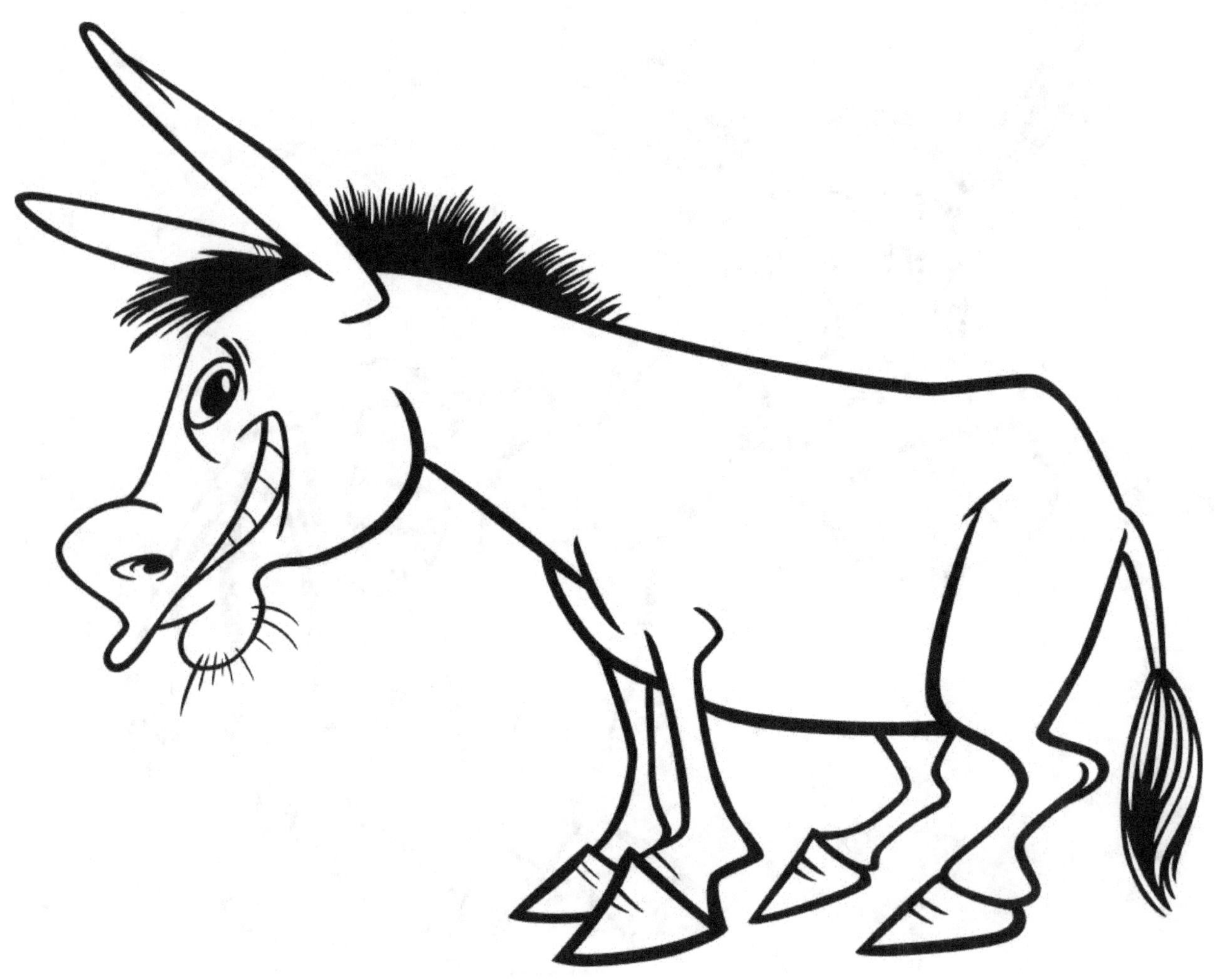

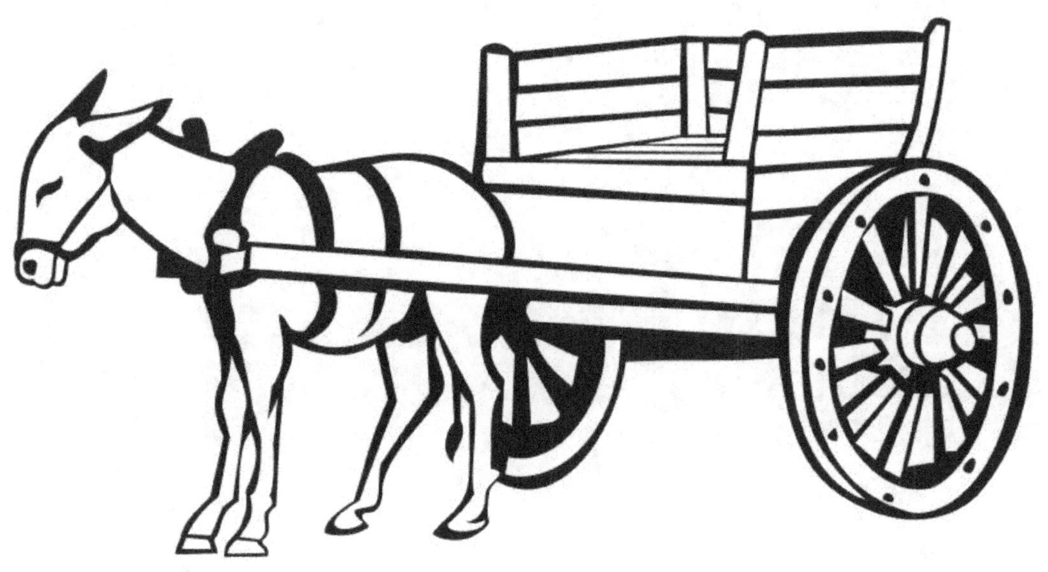

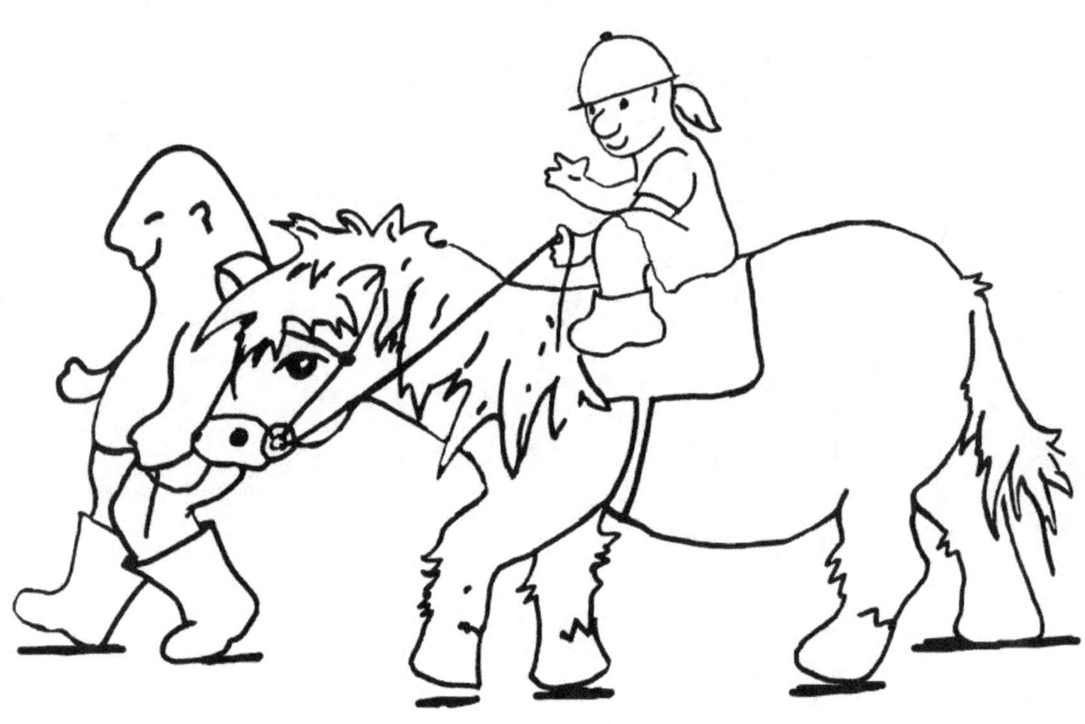

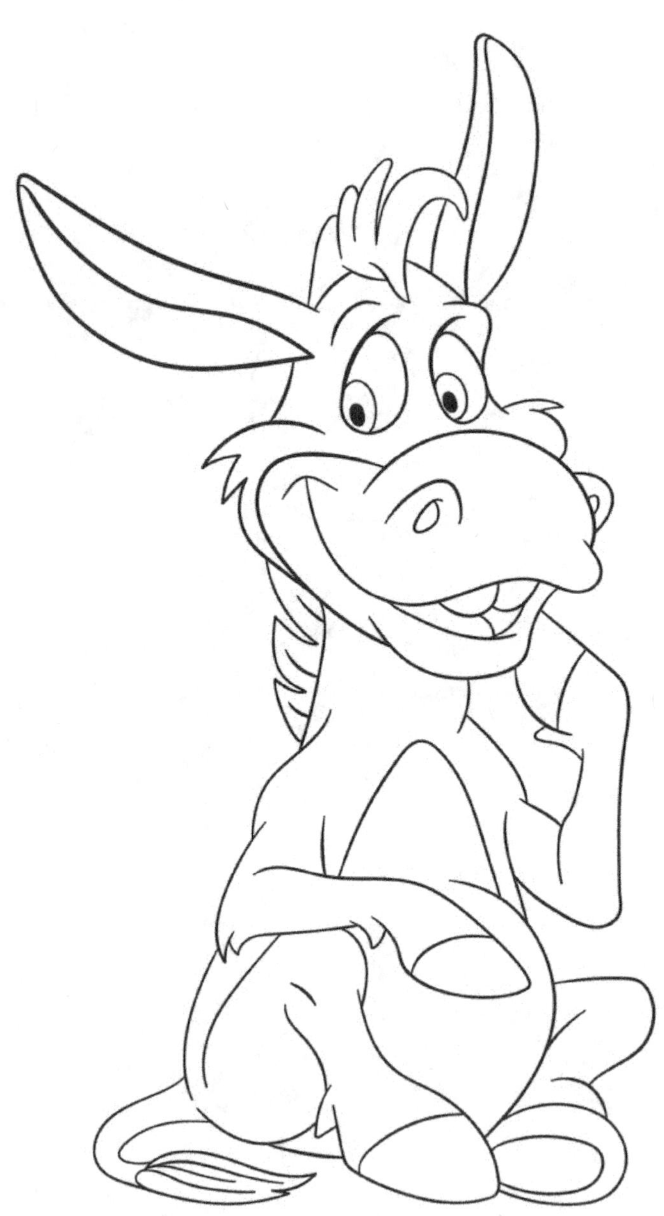

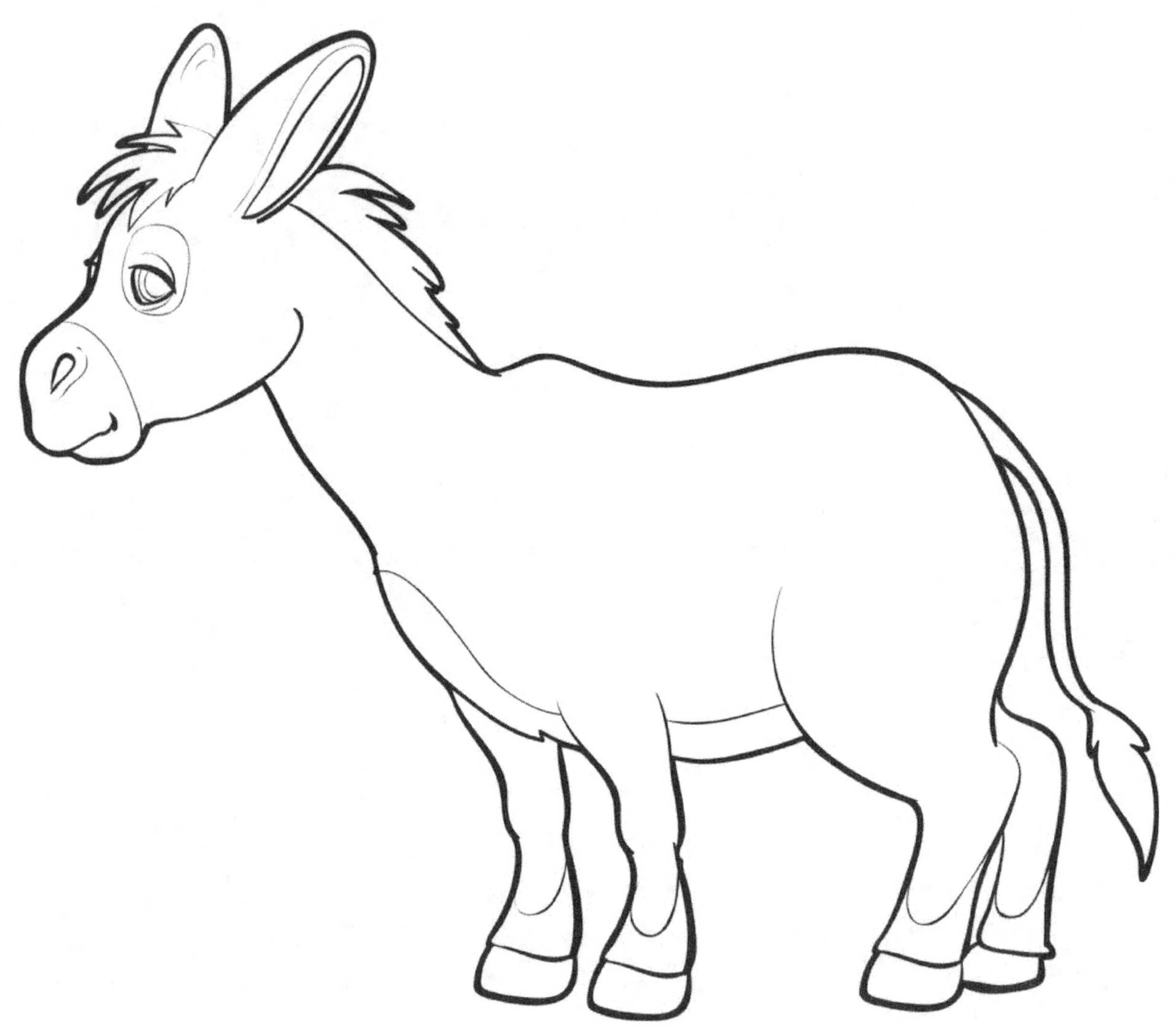

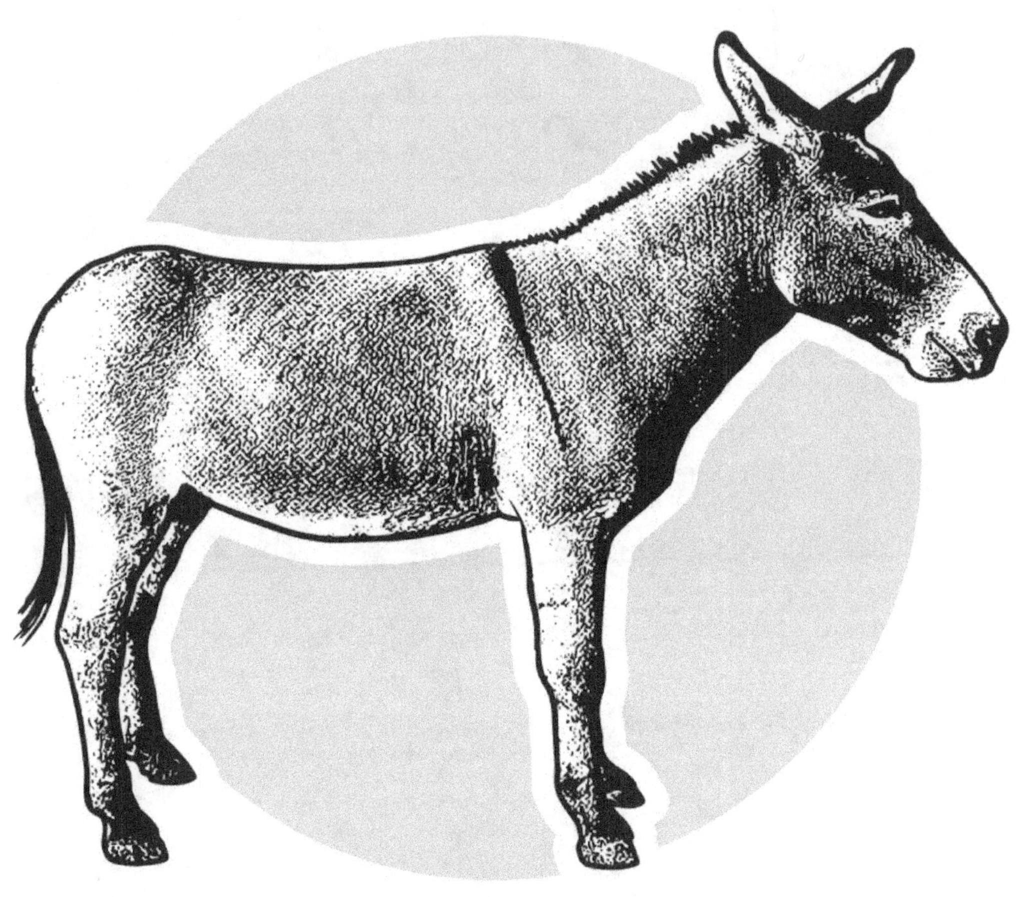

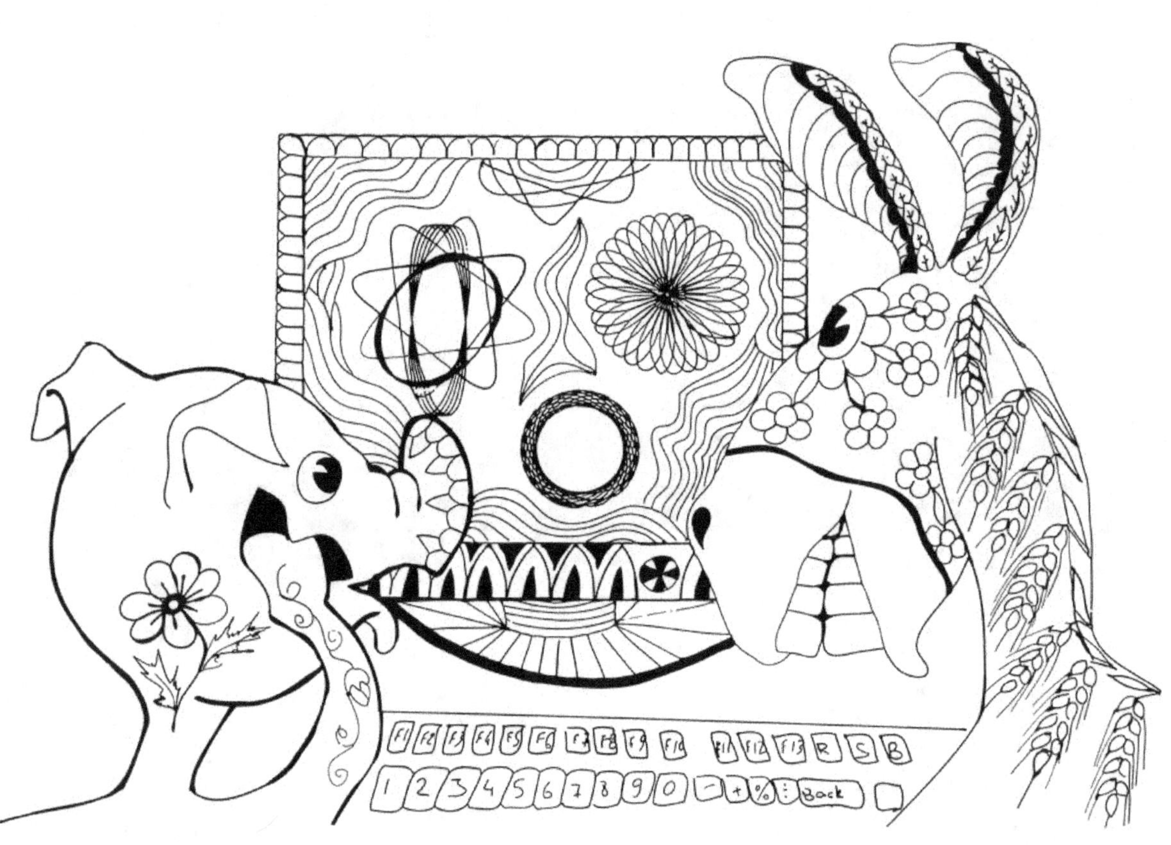

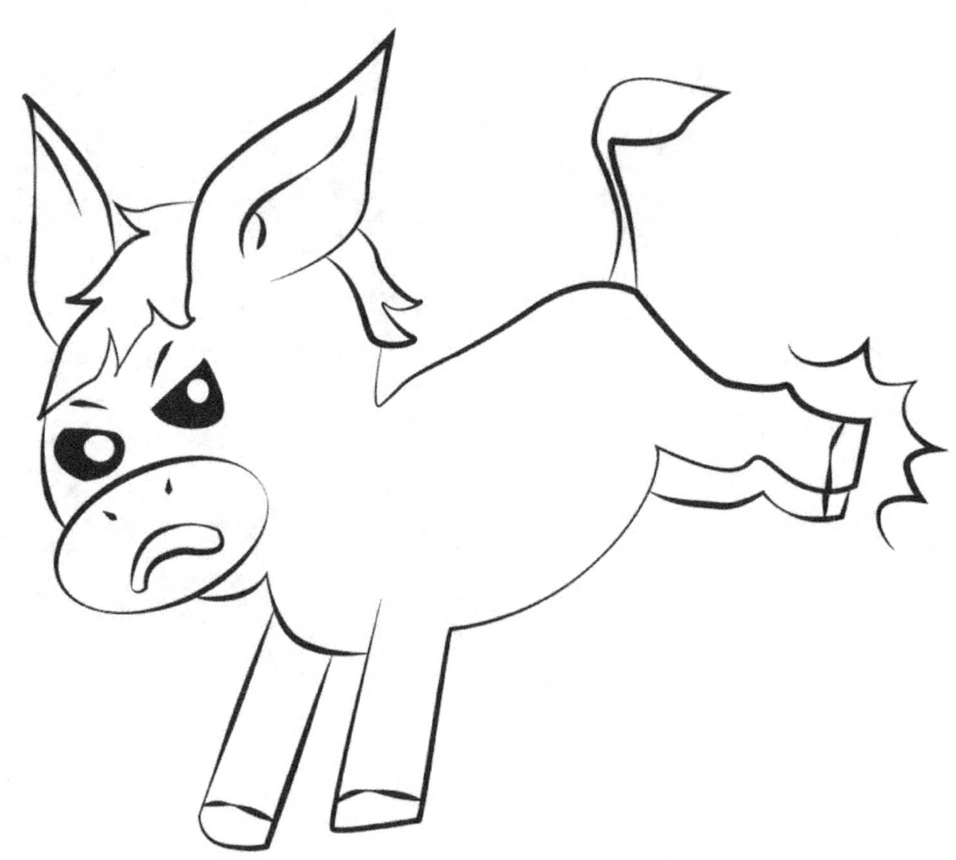

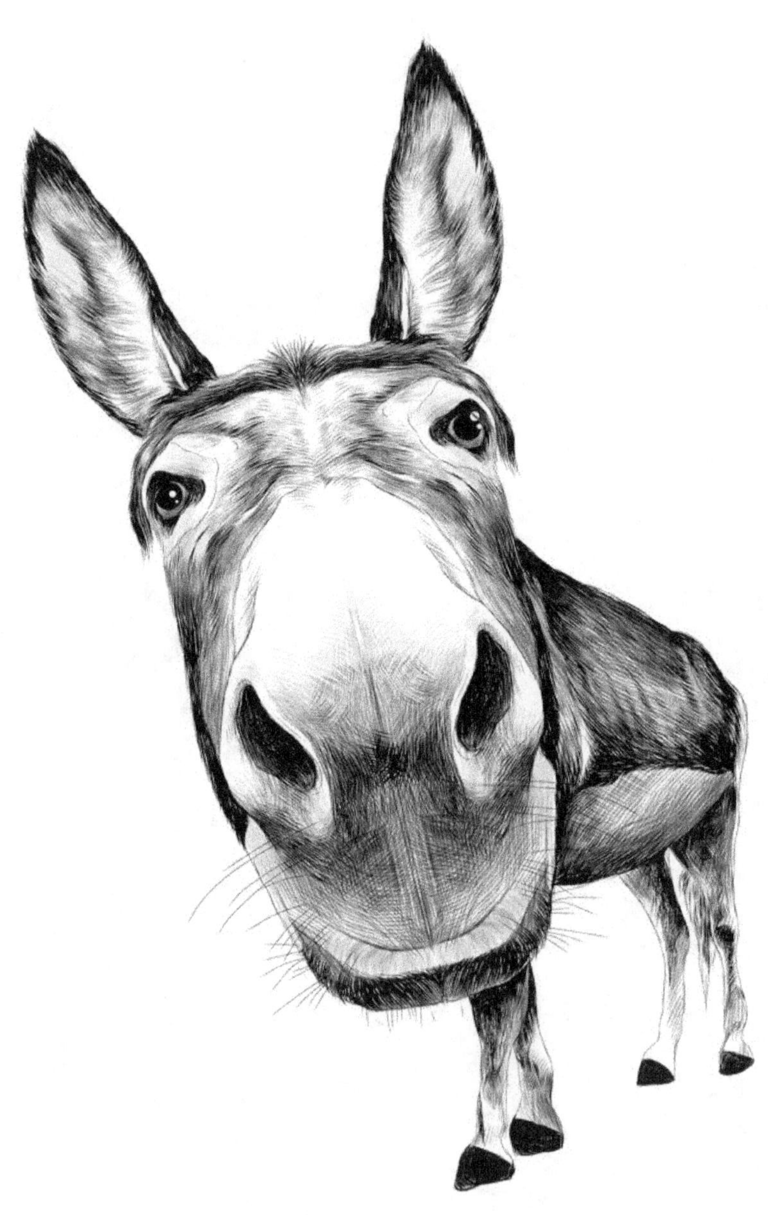

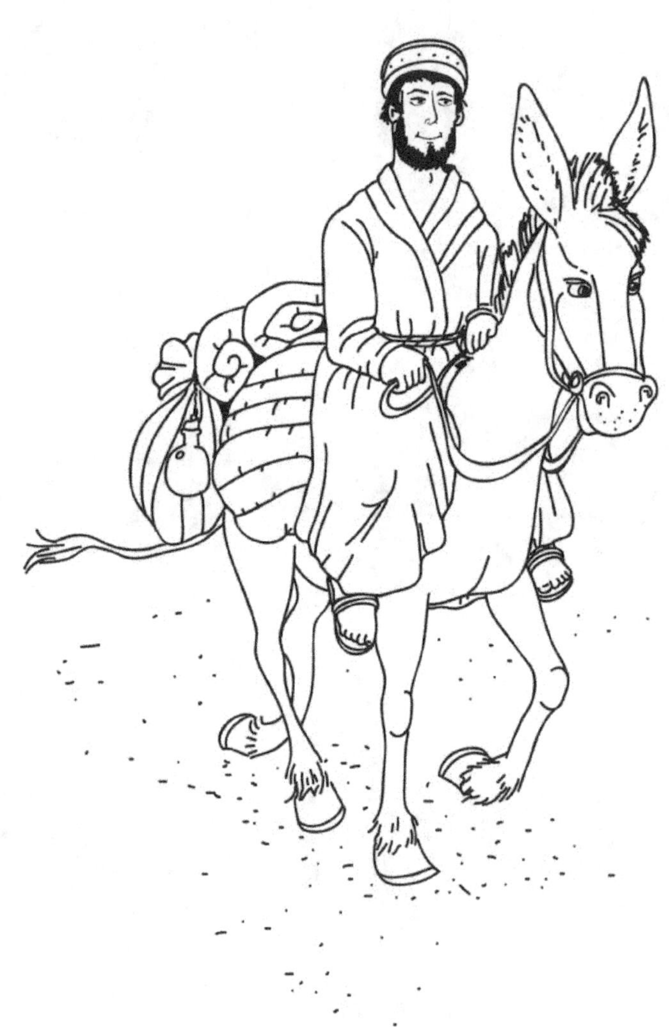

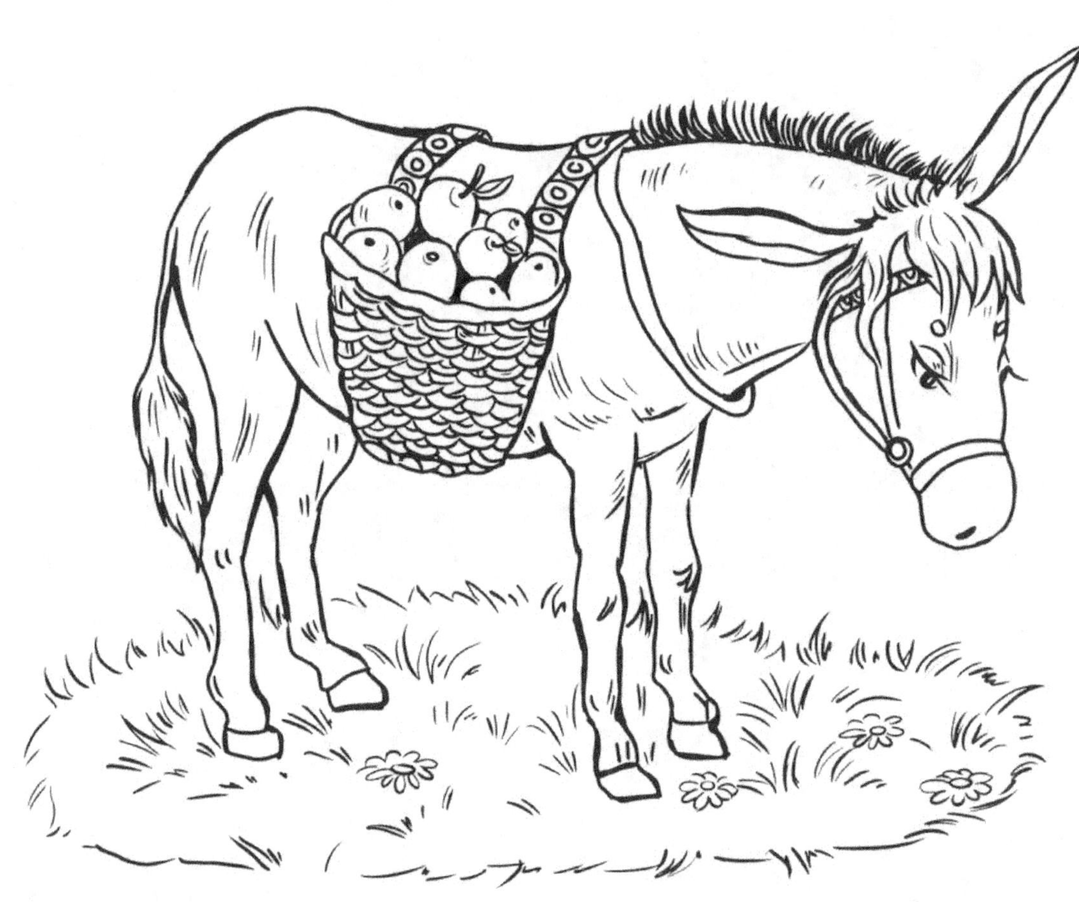

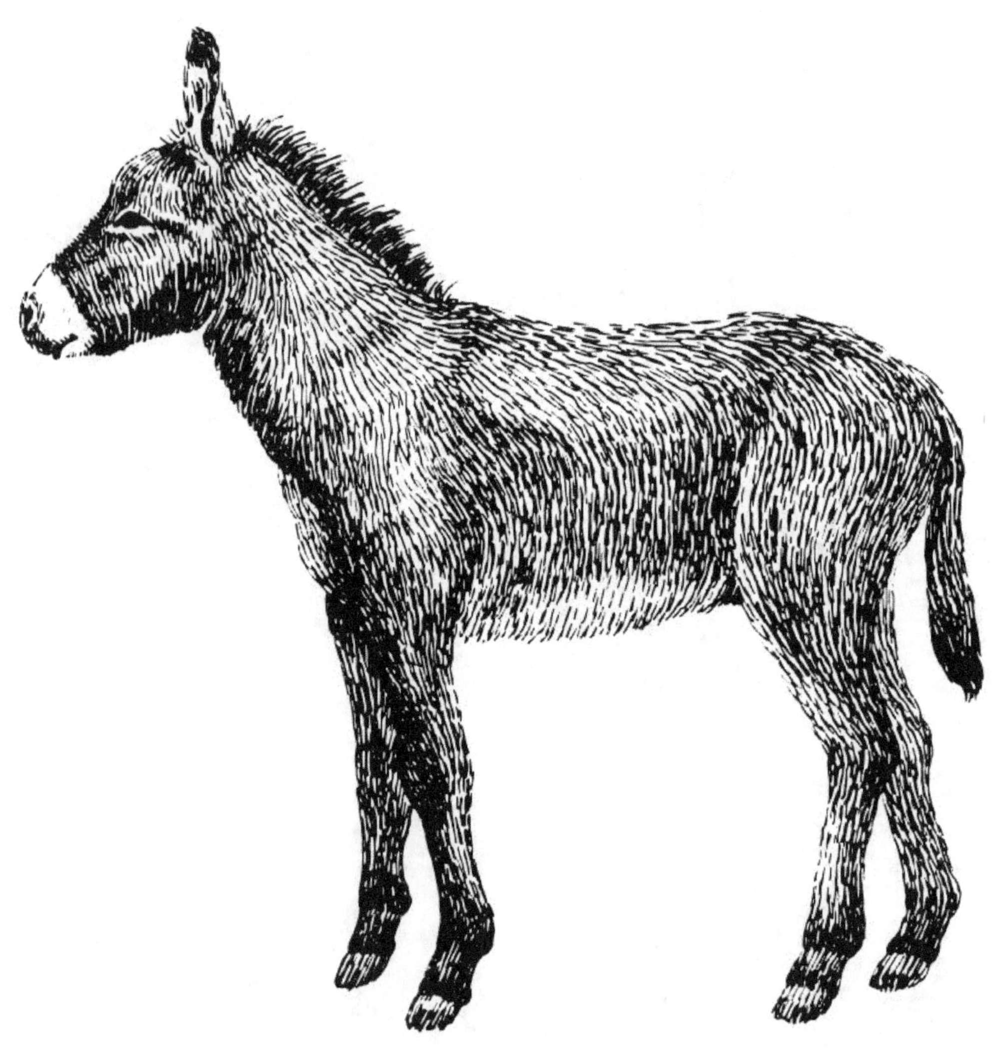

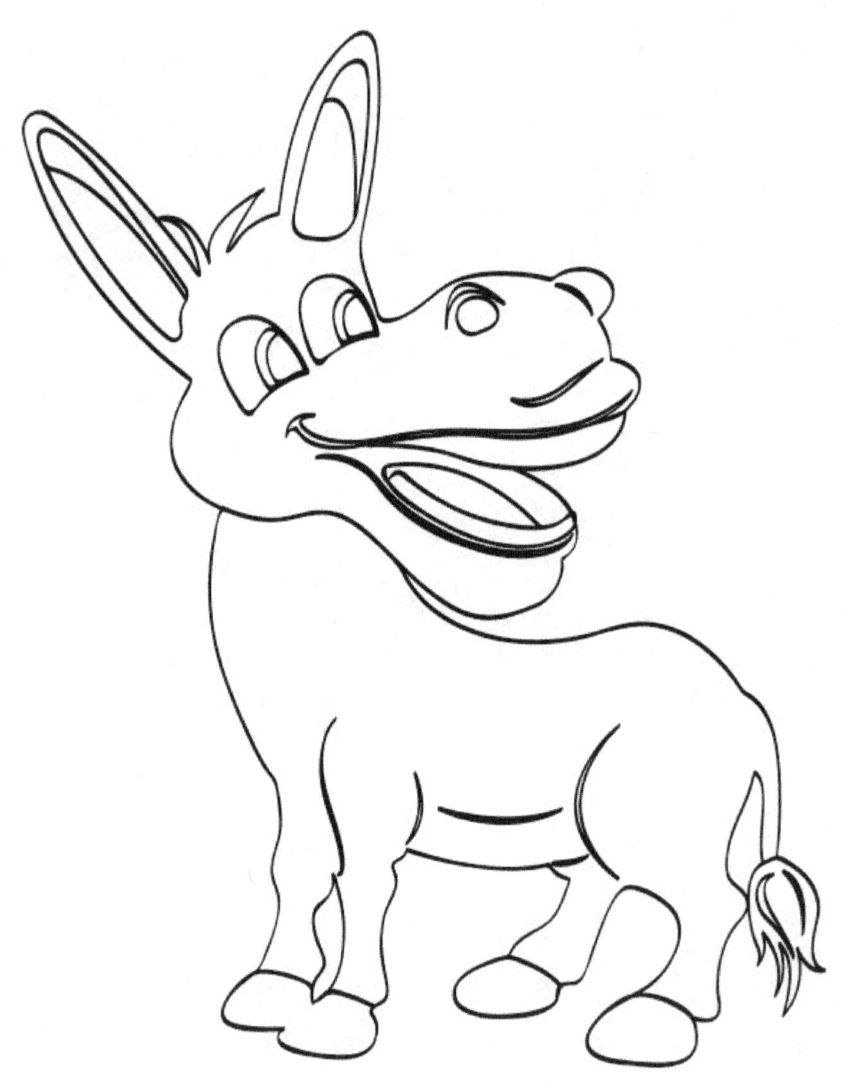

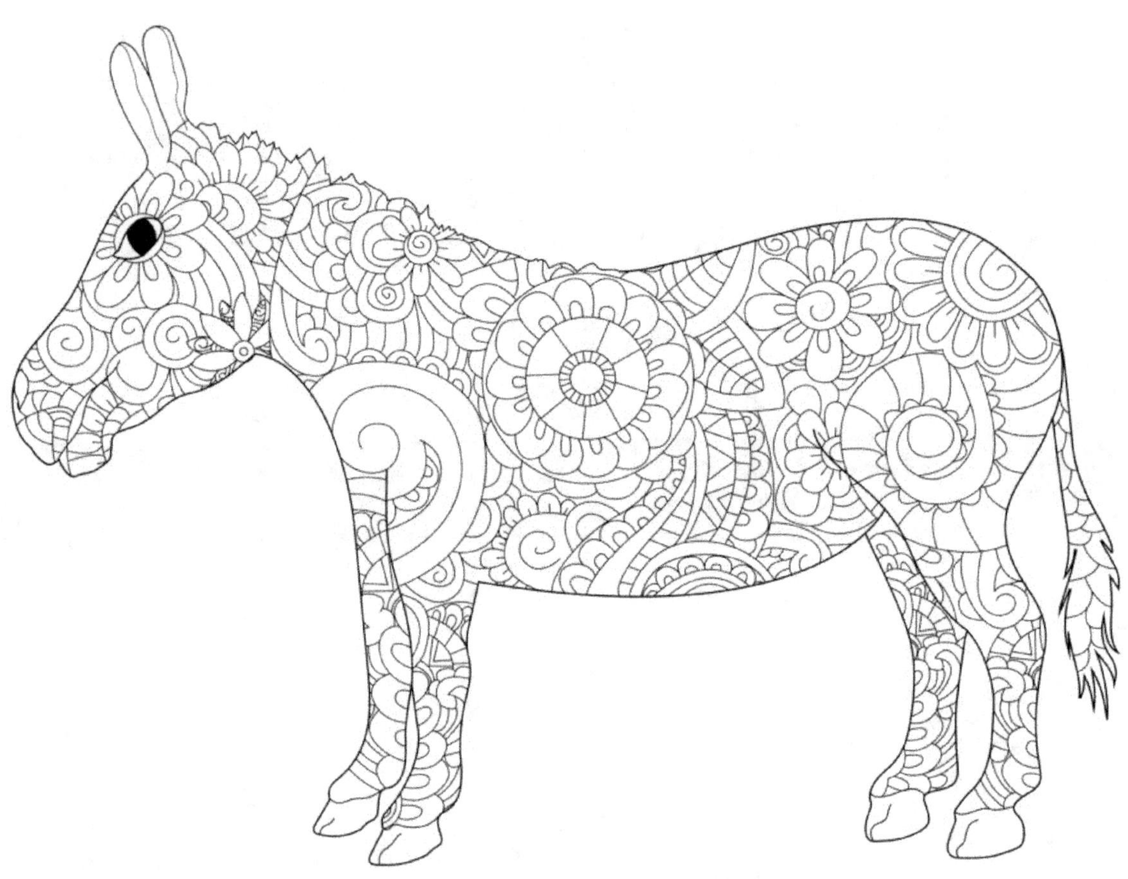

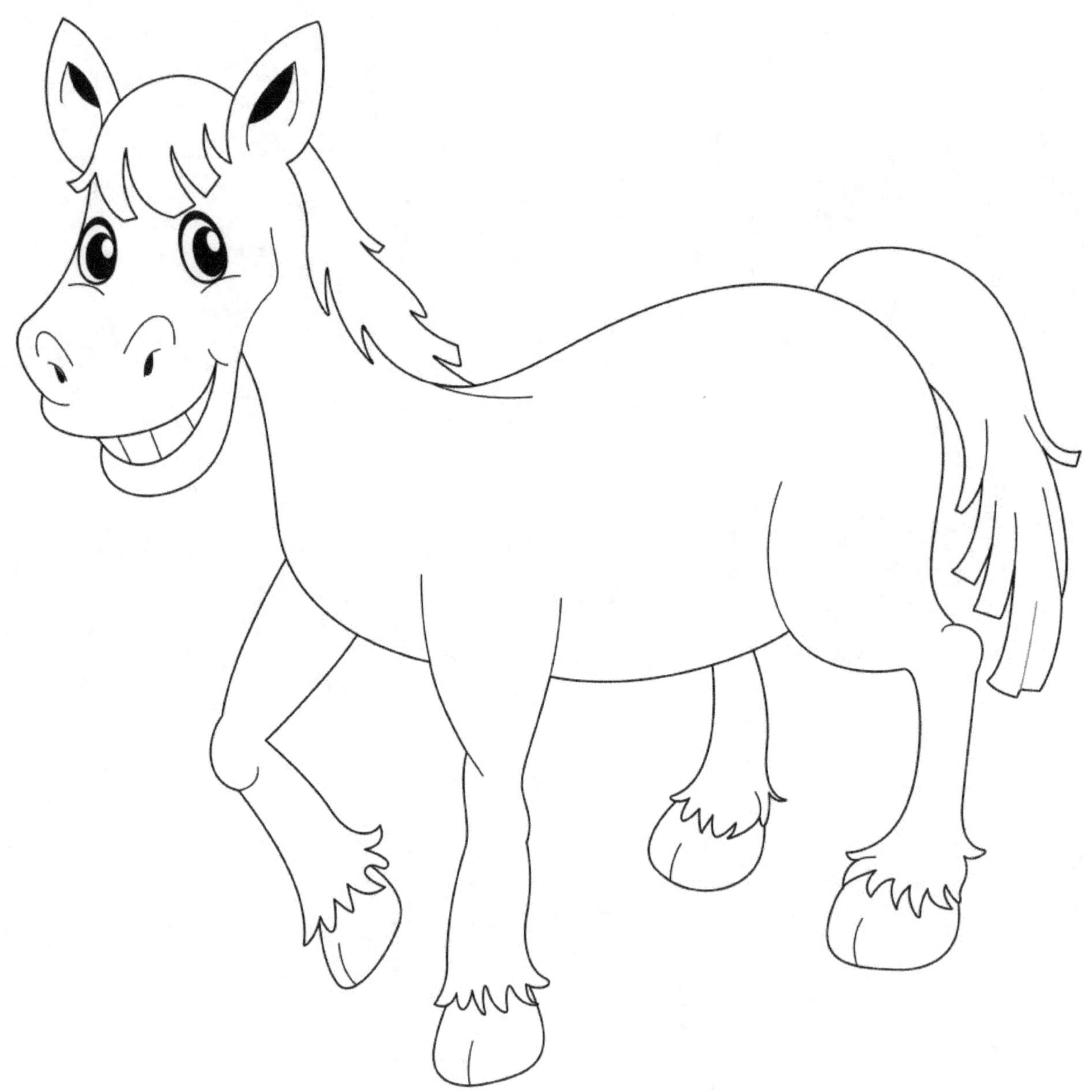

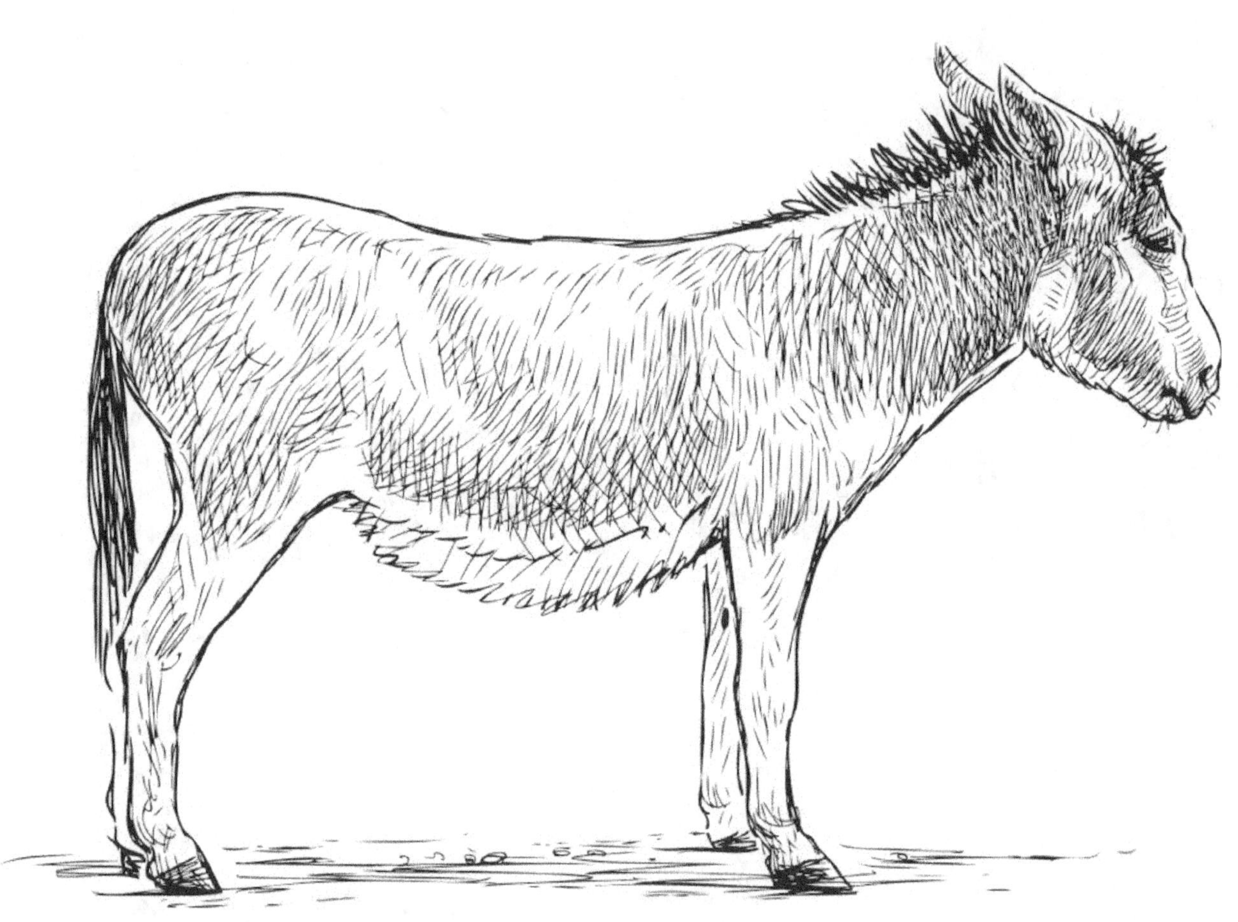

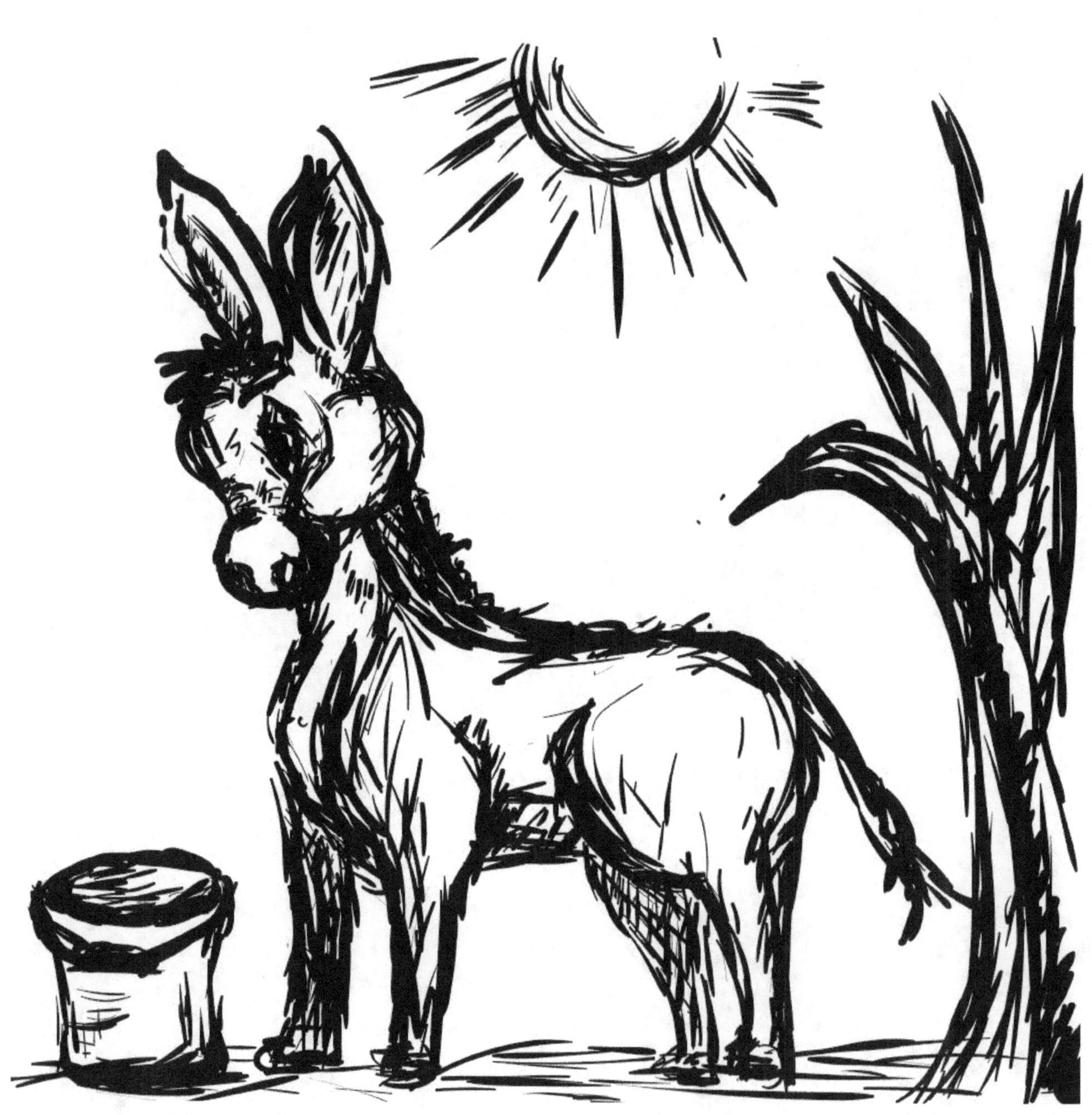

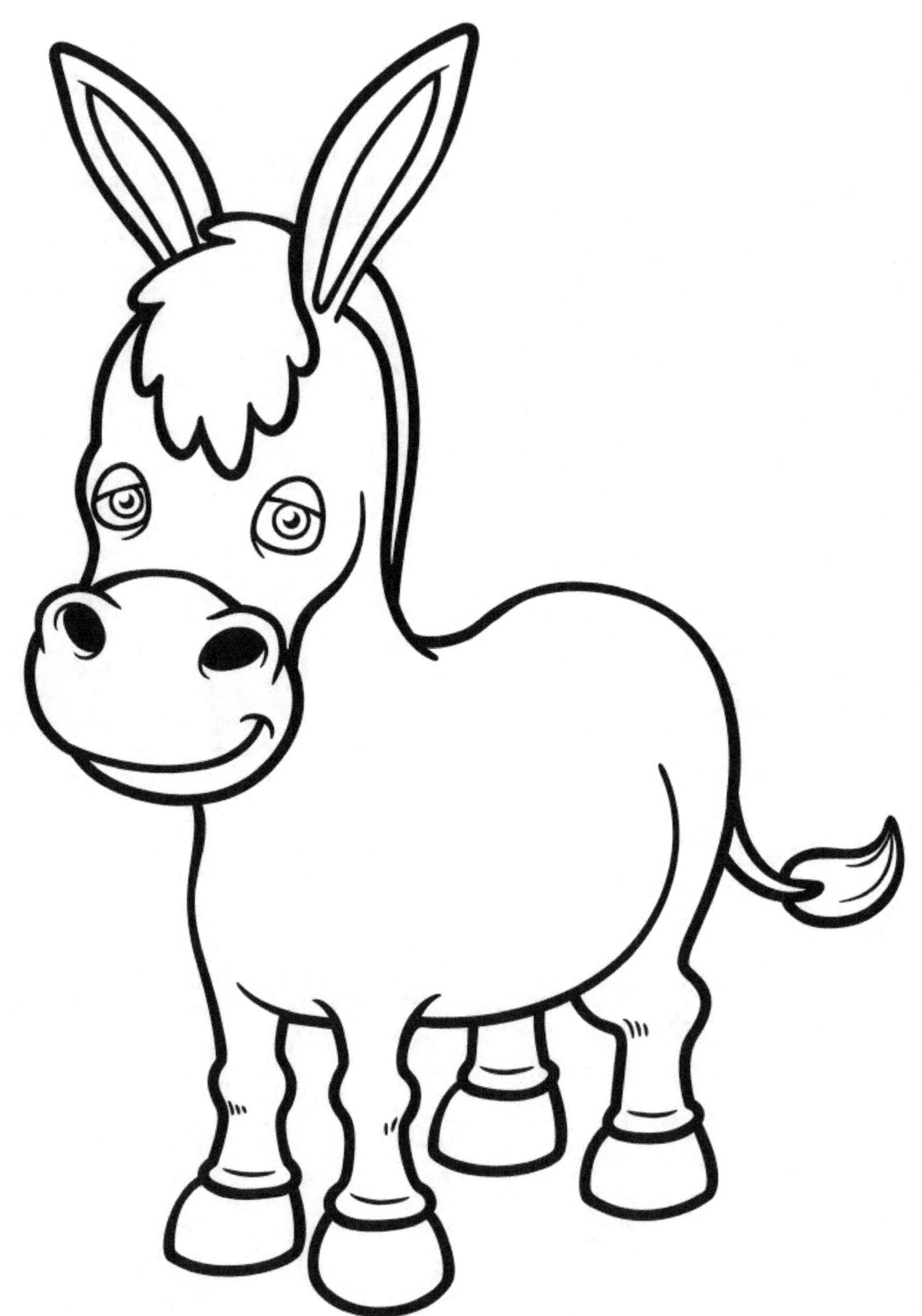

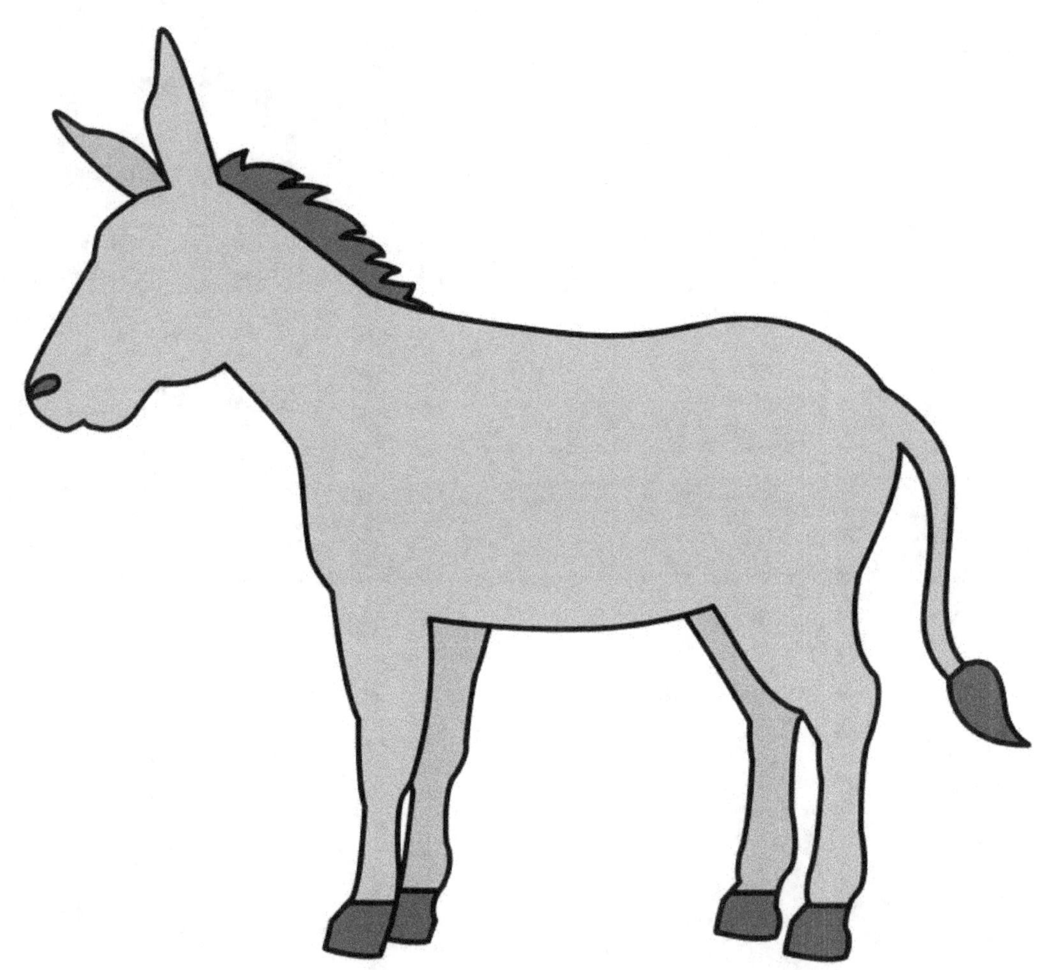

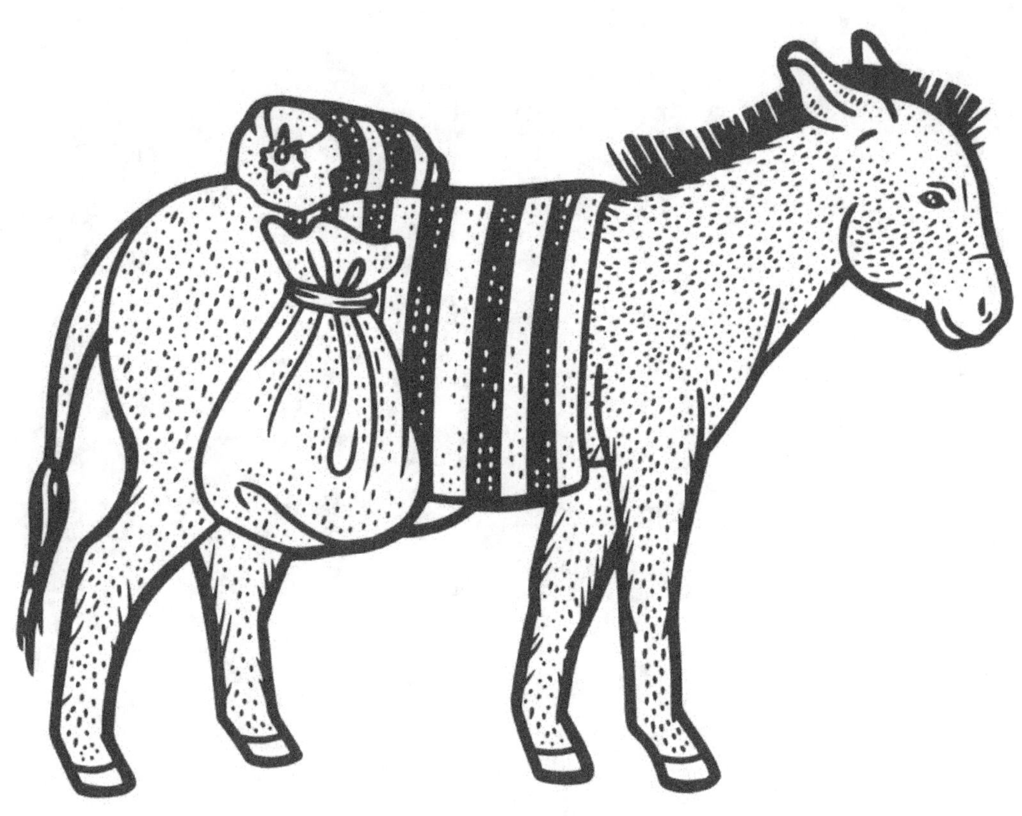

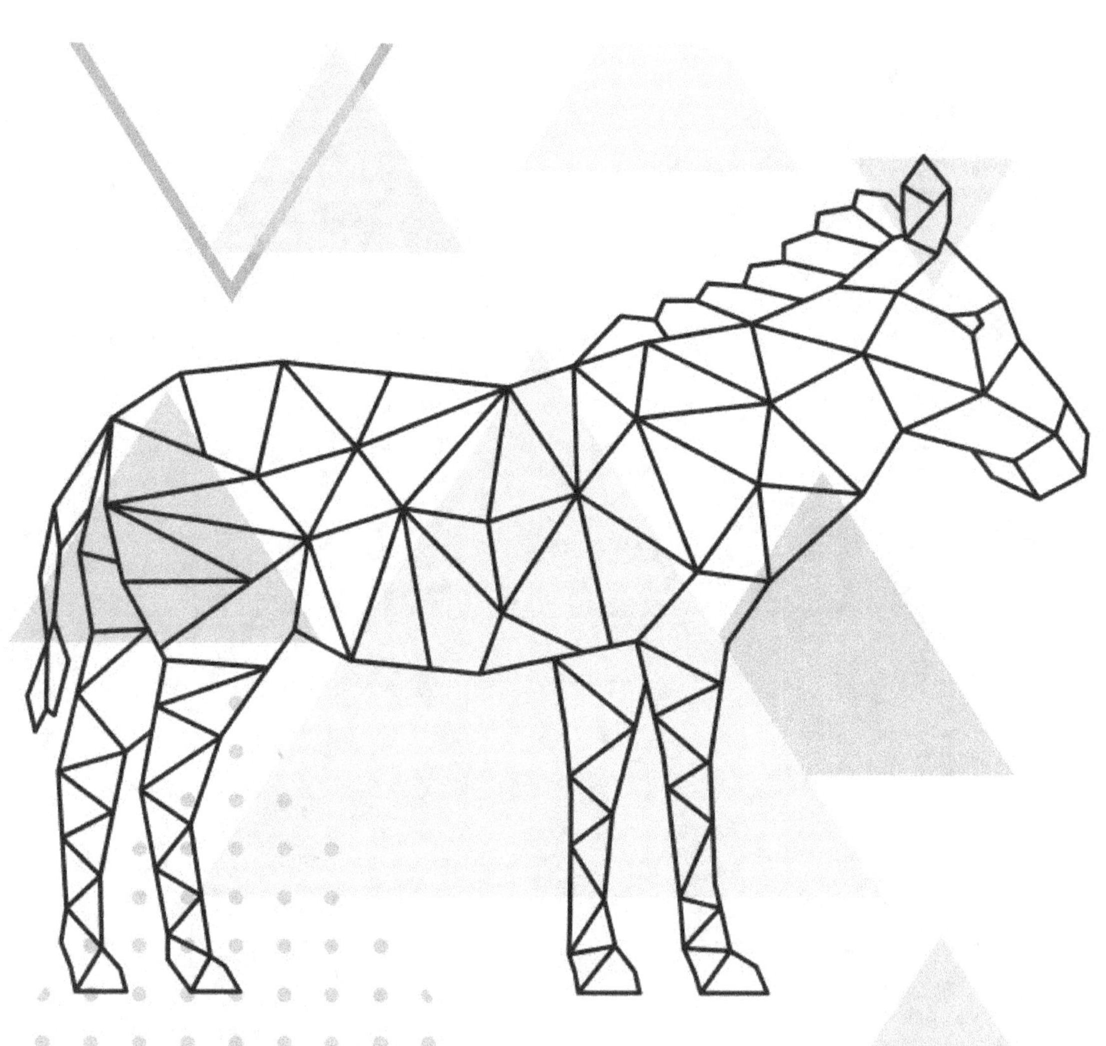

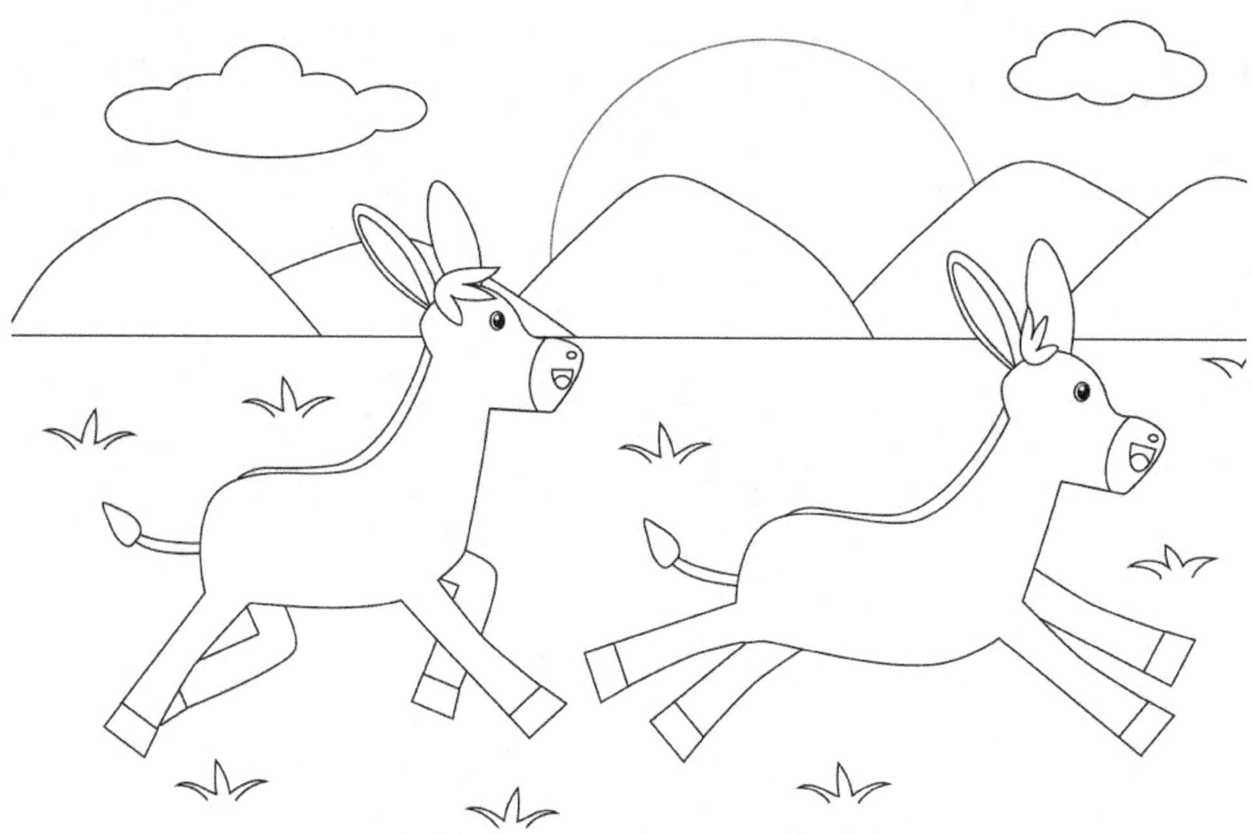

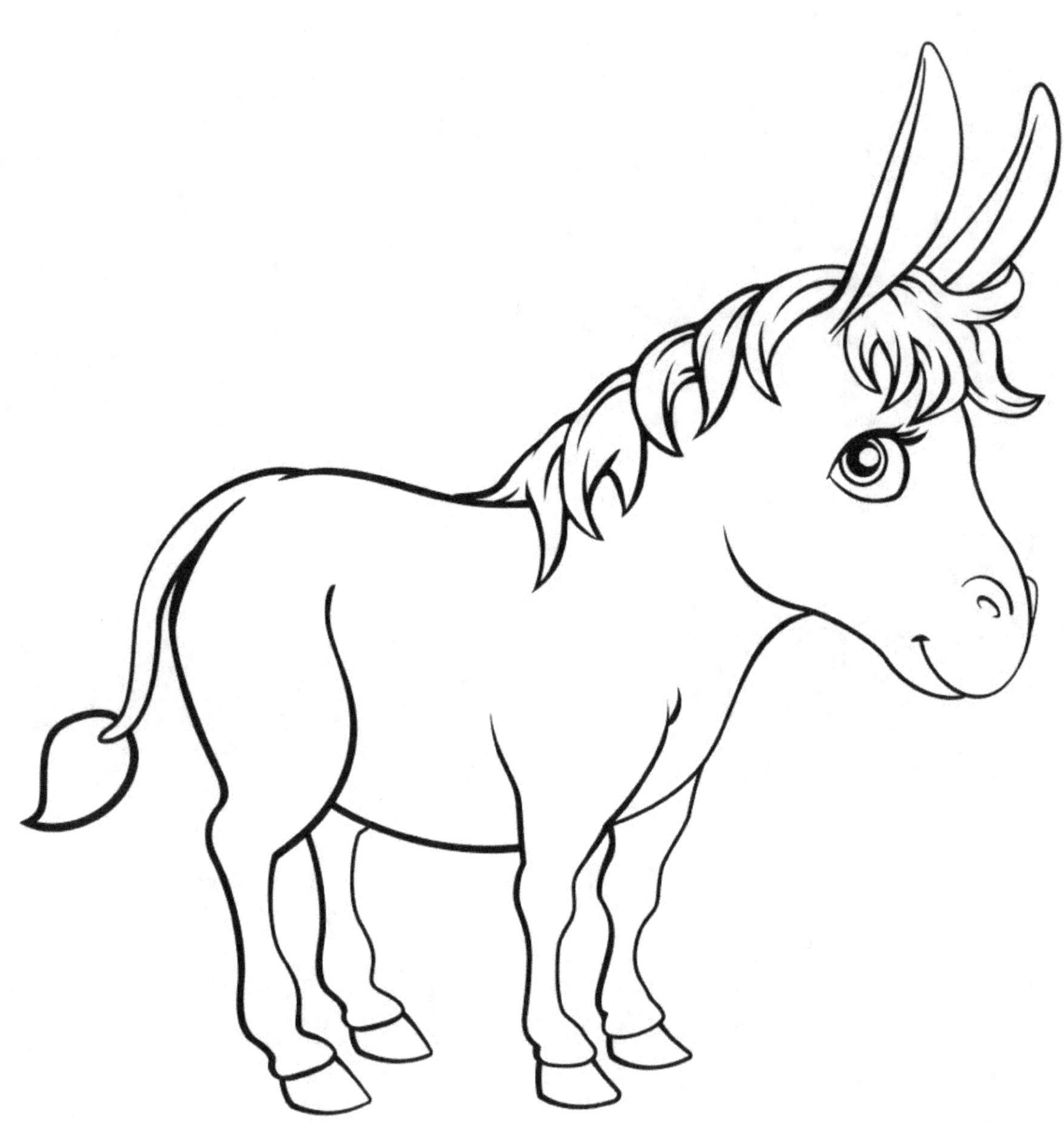

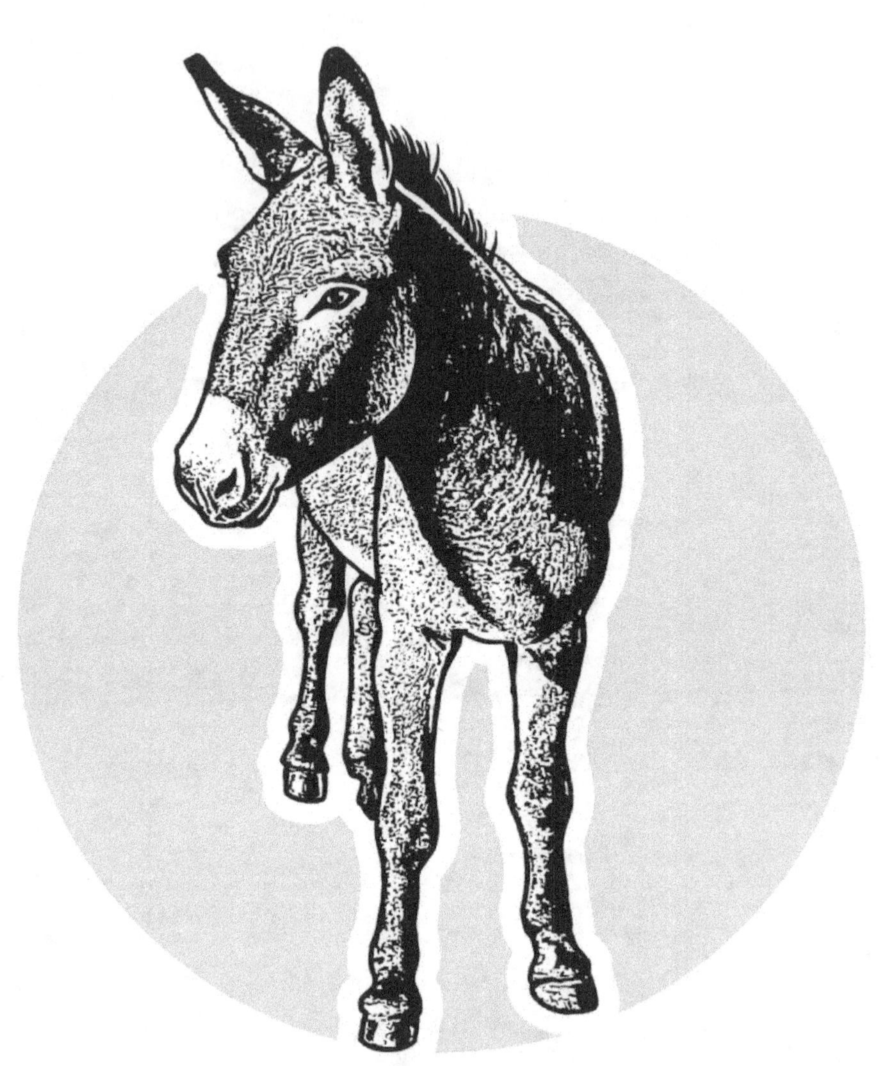

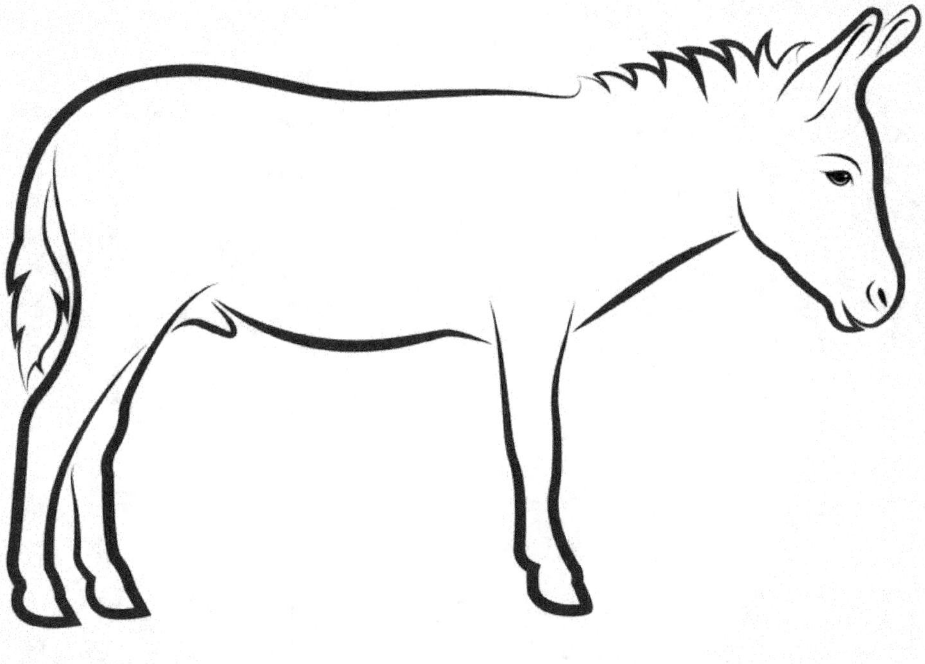

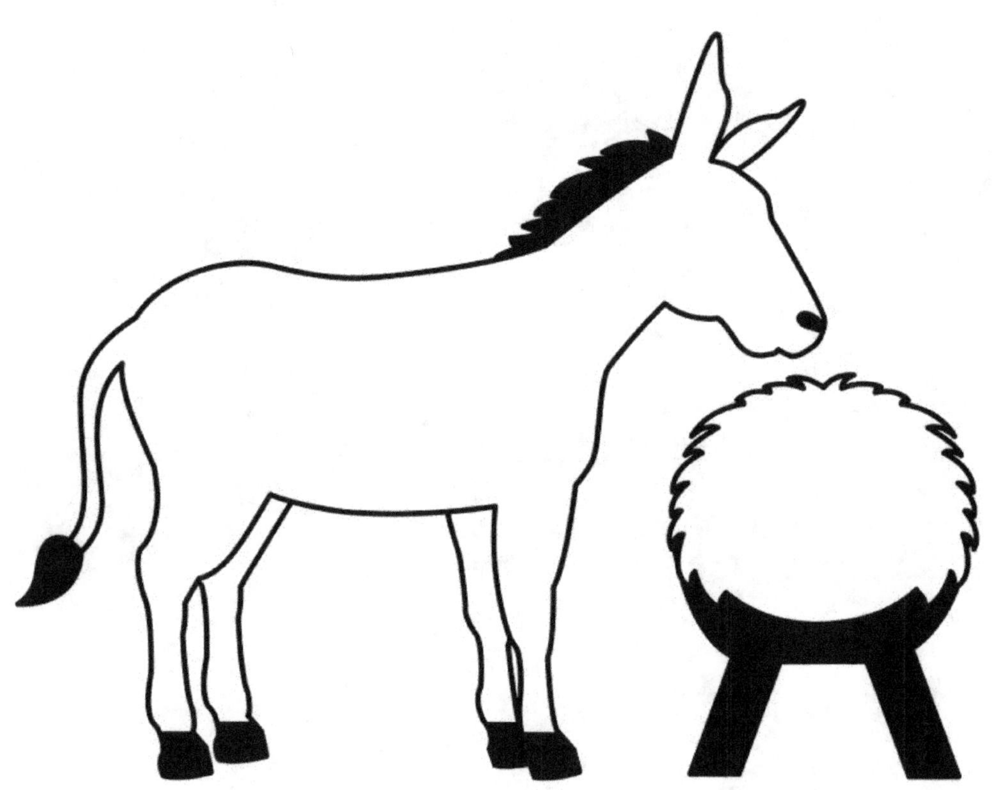

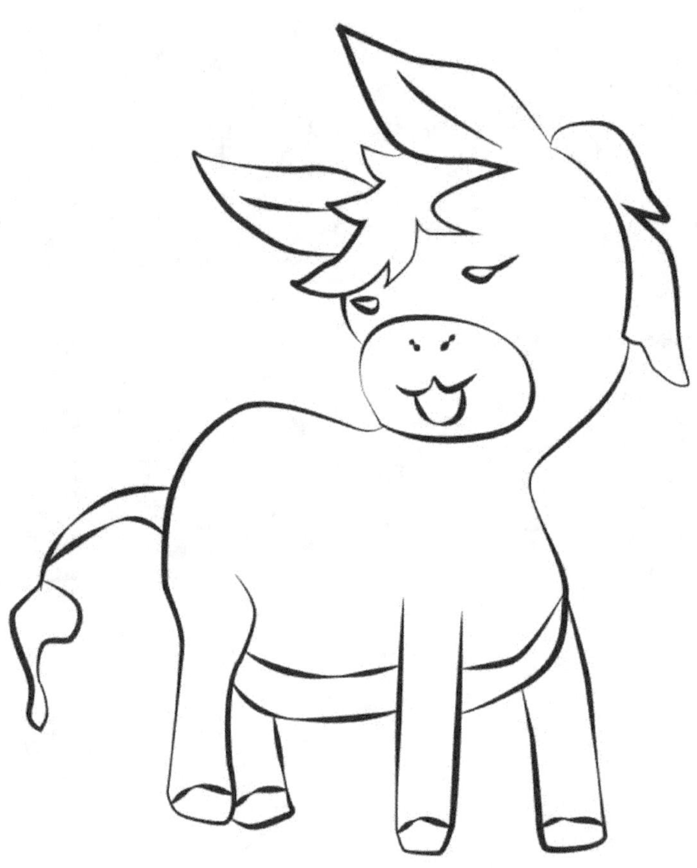

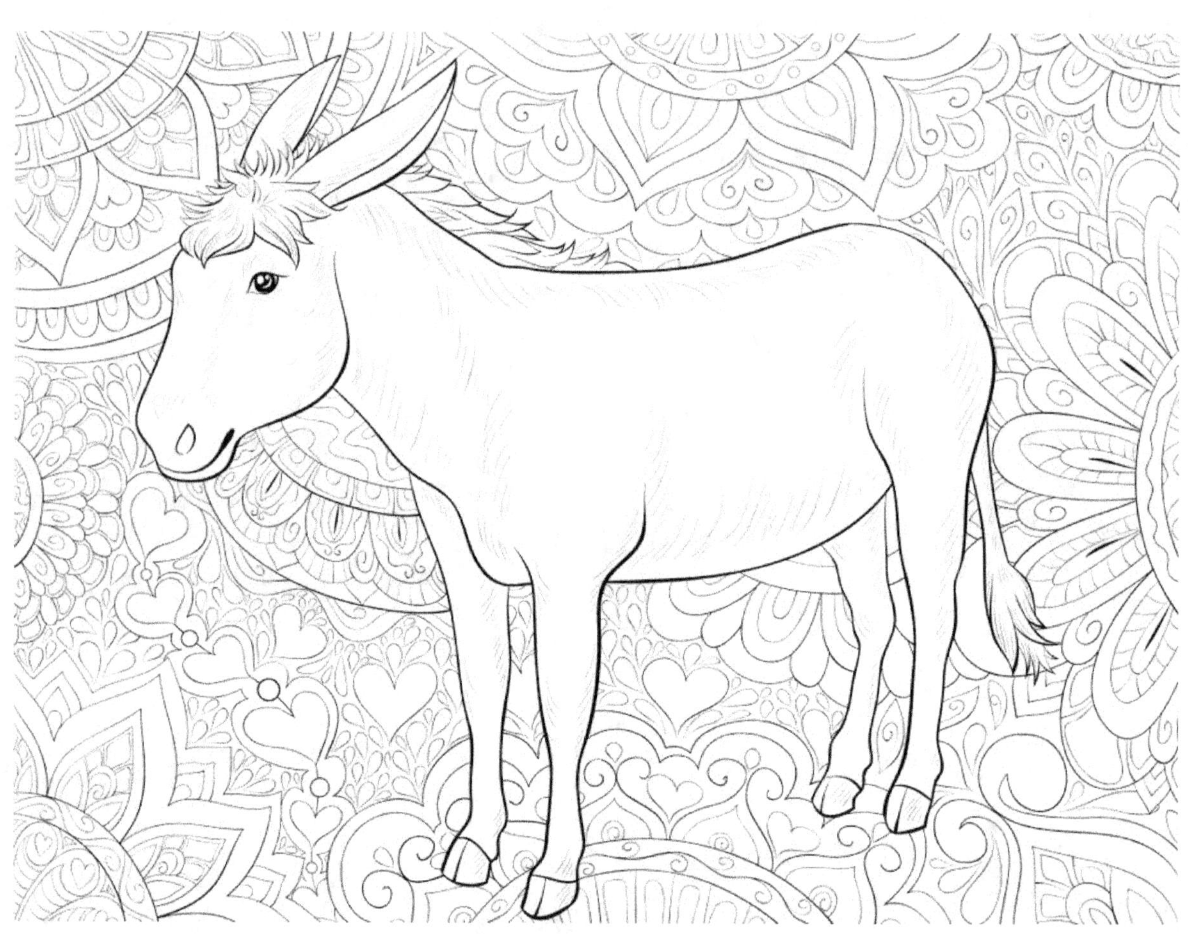

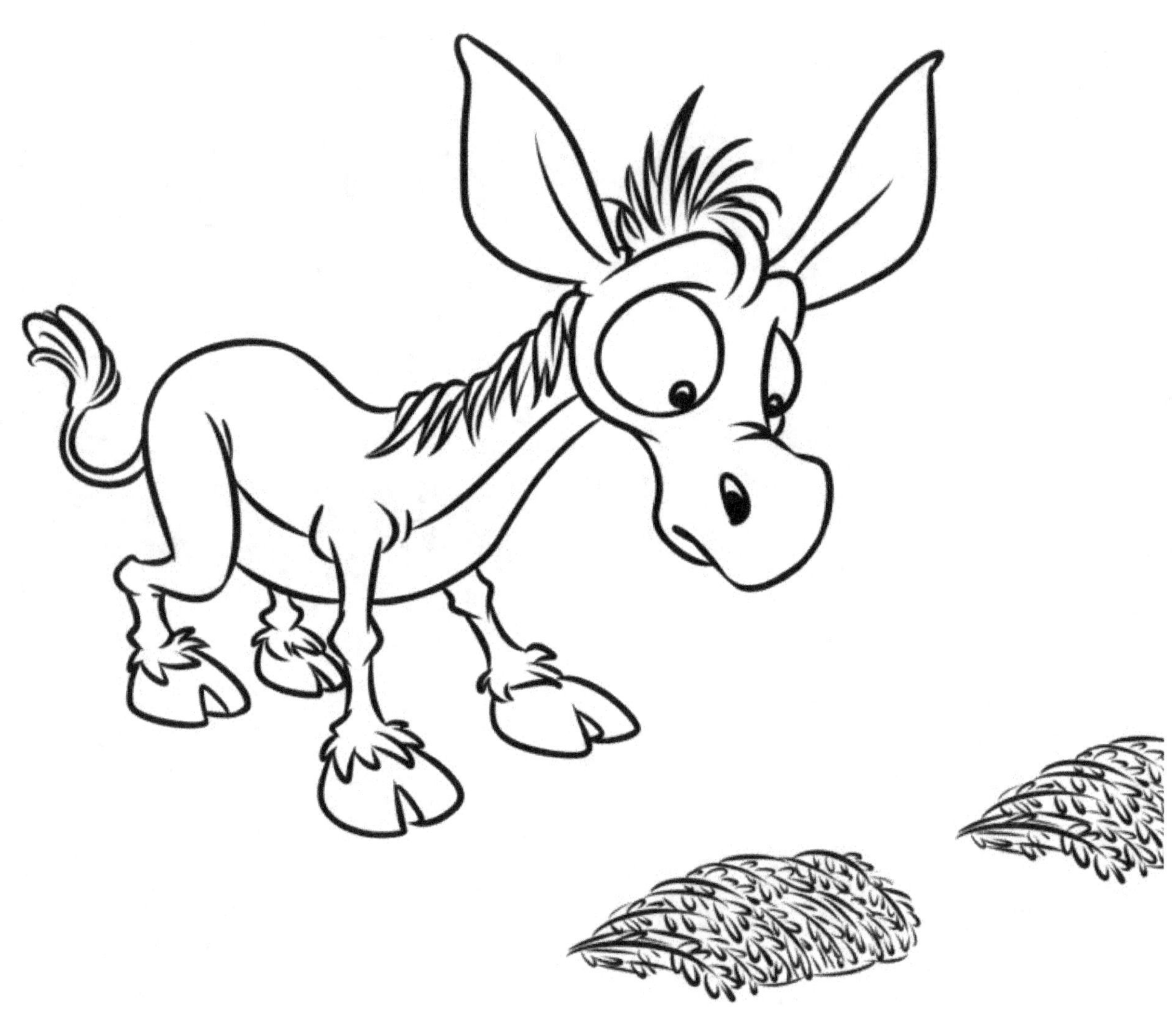

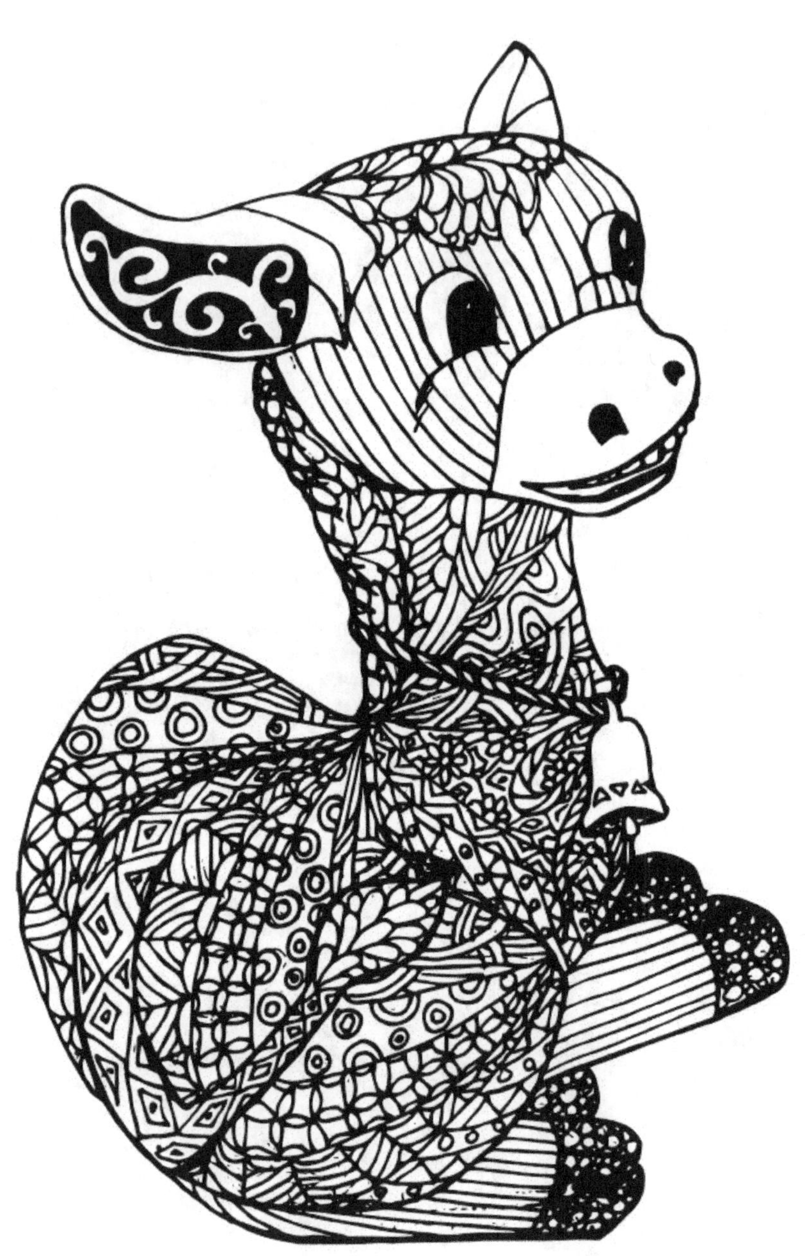

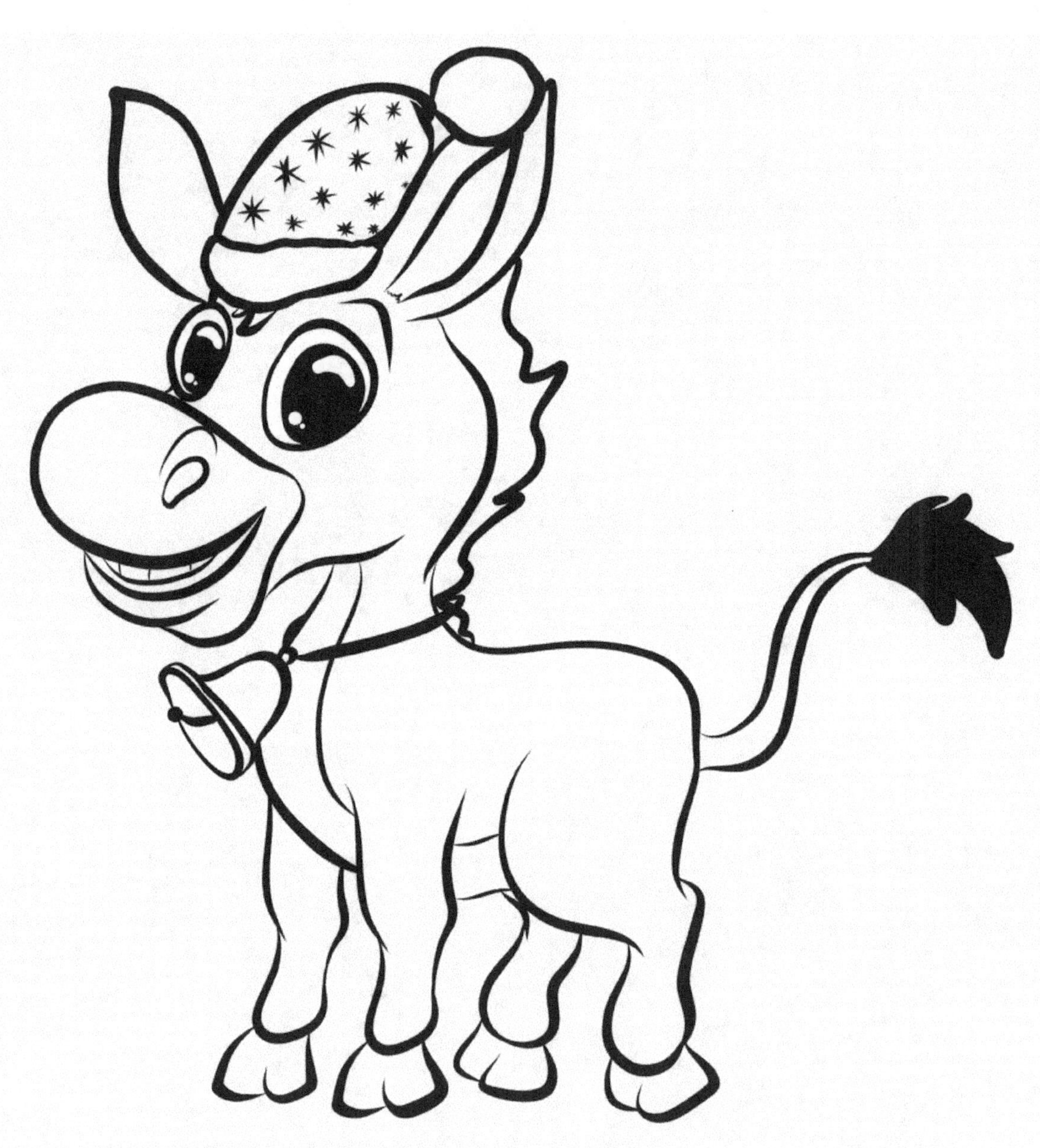

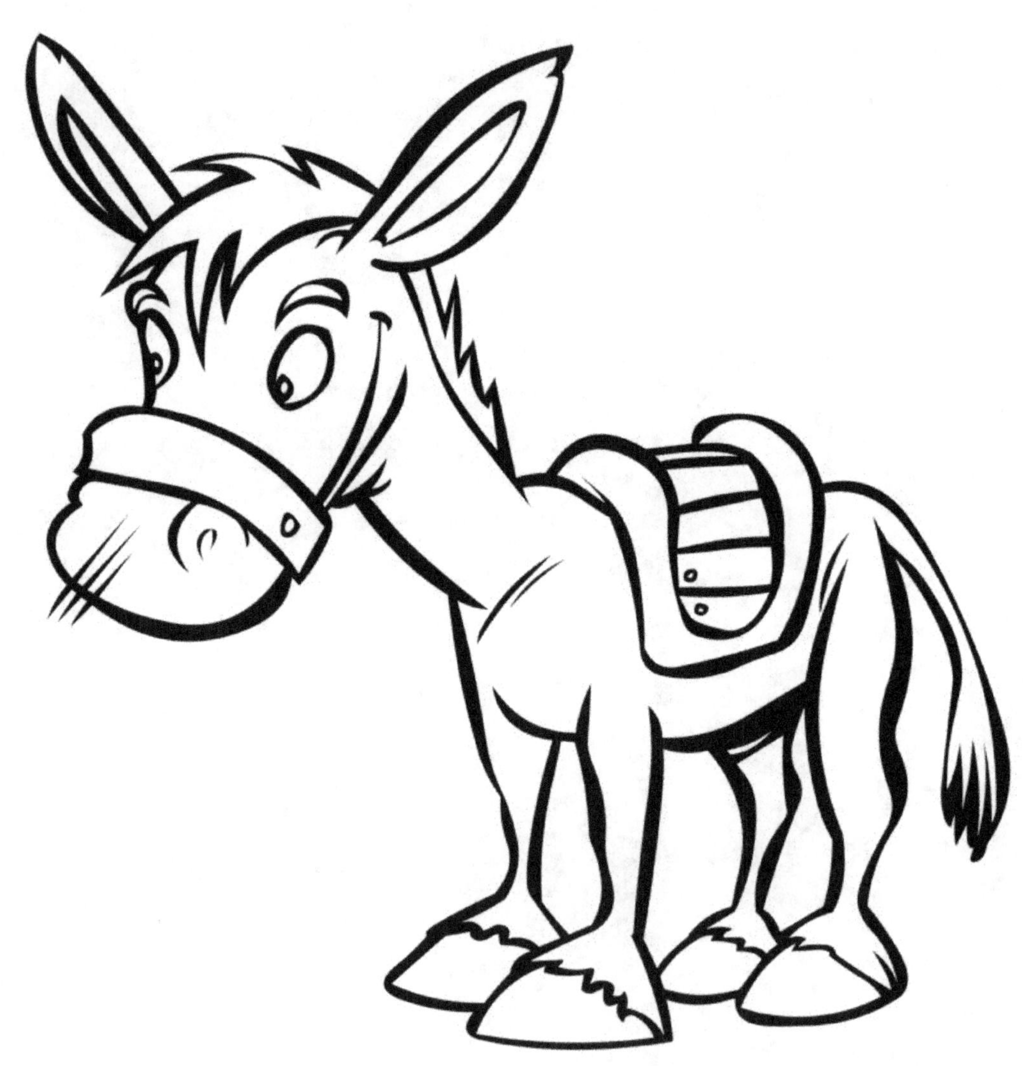